Learning to Love

Learning to Love

Utilizing the Principles and Practices
of Pastoral Care for Mission

SUE M. HOLDSWORTH

Foreword by Steve Taylor

WIPF & STOCK · Eugene, Oregon

LEARNING TO LOVE
Utilizing the Principles and Practices of Pastoral Care for Mission

Copyright © 2024 Sue M. Holdsworth. All rights reserved. Except for brief quotations in critical publications or reviews, no part of this book may be reproduced in any manner without prior written permission from the publisher. Write: Permissions, Wipf and Stock Publishers, 199 W. 8th Ave., Suite 3, Eugene, OR 97401.

Wipf & Stock
An Imprint of Wipf and Stock Publishers
199 W. 8th Ave., Suite 3
Eugene, OR 97401

www.wipfandstock.com

PAPERBACK ISBN: 979-8-3852-2086-1
HARDCOVER ISBN: 979-8-3852-2087-8
EBOOK ISBN: 979-8-3852-2088-5

08/19/24

All Scripture quotations, unless otherwise indicated, are taken from the Holy Bible, New International Version®, NIV®. Copyright ©1973, 1978, 1984, 2011 by Biblica, Inc.™ Used by permission of Zondervan. All rights reserved worldwide. www.zondervan.com The "NIV" and "New International Version" are trademarks registered in the United States Patent and Trademark Office by Biblica, Inc.™

For Julian

Contents

Foreword by Steve Taylor   ix
Preface   xiii
Acknowledgments   xv

PART 1

1. Introduction   3
2. Researching Practice   20
3. Models to Aid Intercultural Care   38
4. Learning to Love   50
5. Major Emerging Themes: Planning and Practicing Intercultural Pastoral Care   73

PART 2

6. Functions of Pastoral Care   81
7. Expressing Love   96
8. Motivations for Service   116
9. Skills for Pastoral Care and Mission   130
10. Mission as Pastoral Care at Church-Based, Intercultural Initiatives   150

Bibliography   169

Foreword

LOVE OF GOD AND love for neighbor is central to *Learning to Love*. Careful research of local churches in community ministry clarifies theology and offers constructive guidance. The result is a book reframing how local churches can love their neighbors with integrity.

Learning to Love is grounded in real life: first, the experiences of Dr. Holdsworth as a migrant; second, years of service for a mission agency, during which she saw the (at times clumsy) attempts by local churches to connect with their neighbors. These years of experience raised questions for Dr. Holdsworth. How do contemporary churches connect with communities? How might theologies, values, and attitudes be integrated to express authentic witness to Christian faith?

Dr. Holdsworth seeks answers with and from migrants. Choosing four local churches, she carefully observes how they are learning to love. She sits in English classes and observes how volunteers teach. She participates in newcomers' events and watches who talks with whom about what. She interviews volunteers about their motivations. She attends leadership planning meetings and shares in worship to understand how theologies preached can inform local mission. Such is the power of ethnography, as it seeks to understand the perspectives of those observed, in this case, how local churches are learning to love.

Weaving lived experience with Scripture and theology, *Learning to Love* constructs a practical theology of volunteering—or what Dr. Holdsworth calls "grace in action."

Grace in action involves evangelism, defined as a person-centered approach that offers others the possibility of "experiencing God's holiness" (120). Perceptions of evangelism as using words and needing to result in conversion have proven detrimental. Instead, the research shows how valuing genuine and long-term friendships creates safe, positive, and fruitful environments. What results is evangelism that is "truthful, clear, and incarnated" (122).

Grace in action involves pastoral care, understood as hospitality given, received, and mutually shared. Dr. Holdsworth gently challenges the individualism of Western care paradigms and provides shared resources that across cultures can form how ordinary people love their neighbors with integrity.

Grace in action is a local spirituality for mission, "mature, reasoned, compassionate demonstrations of God's love" (12) that emerge from practices of faith, prayer, and reflective action.

As I read *Learning to Love*, I kept thinking about Velcro, the plastic strips with small hooks that together strengthen connections. *Learning to Love* offers wisdom to strengthen the "Velcro" of church-based ministry. Every community-based initiative involves countless little actions—a smile of welcome, a listening ear, and an interest to learn.

For volunteers, this book provides concrete suggestions for enhancing care through supervision, accountable relationships, spiritual direction, and culturally relevant spiritual disciplines.

For leaders of church-based initiatives, this book gives ideas for team meetings and ways to apply frameworks like Cultural Intelligence, Theological Action Research, systems thinking, storytelling, and circles of trust.

For ministers and those who preach and lead worship, this book shows what integrating visionary words and practical actions means.

For policymakers, this book underlines the importance of church-based initiatives in the social fabric of local communities and the potential of on-the-job training and reflective practice.

The book offers countless constructive suggestions to strengthen the "Velcro" of community ministry. The result is a practical theology rooted in love: love of God and neighbor. It is a rich feast of wisdom gleaned from careful attention to the grounded realities, salted with years of reflection on the nature of Christian ministry and mission.

I wish I had *Learning to Love* when I began in congregational ministry. One of the first people I met while church planting in Auckland, New Zealand, was David,[1] a recently arrived migrant from China. As well as planting a church, I was also a caretaker at the nearby theology college. Locking up the library one winter night, David knocked on the door. In

---

1. Name changed to ensure confidentiality.

halting English, David insisted he needed something photocopied. And to be baptized.

Walking home for dinner, I pondered the conversation. I had helped David with photocopying, but why would a migrant ask about baptism at a library? Was he photocopying a birth certificate? Was he mispronouncing the name of what was a Baptist theology college? Or was something spiritual at play?

A few days later, I was telling my wife about this strange encounter. As we talked, I suddenly saw David ride past on his bike. "That's him!" I yelled. David biked around the corner and I followed at a jog.

That was how I met David. We realized that baptism was his way of expressing a desire to join a church. Over the years, we helped David and his family move house. We offered them conversational English. We prayed for their children through sickness. I was young in ministry, and *Learning to Love* would have given me tools to enhance my intercultural care.

A few years later, the church plant initiated a monthly church service that offered a simple English sermon and opportunities for connection across cultures. To encourage connections, we taught people to greet each other in different languages. As the minister, wanting to lead by example, I approached a young man and offered a greeting in Korean. "Oh, I don't speak Korean," he replied in excellent English. My stereotyping by skin color had closed my eyes to the complexity of second-generation migrant experiences. *Learning to Love*, with its many constructive suggestions, would have provided resources to develop the leaders of this unfolding intercultural ministry.

Dr. Holdsworth is a skilled observer and a deep thinker. She is also a solution provider, offering a constructive road map for all churches involved in a church-based community ministry. Where there is a lack of faith sharing, *Learning to Love* provides processes to enhance prayer and encourage authentic sharing. Where there is poor behavior and the need for cultural awareness, the book offers practical group exercises. Where there are unhelpful theologies, *Learning to Love* invites on-the-job learning from migrants.

Learning to Love is not a book of blue sky dreaming or ten impossible practices before dawn. It is a book about the nature of neighborhood mission, the shape of community care, and resources that can empower grace in action for hundreds of everyday congregations and thousands of ordinary people.

FOREWORD

I thank Dr. Holdsworth for her commitment to integrating the love of God and neighbor. I am grateful to the four churches willing to be researched and to every volunteer who takes the time to care. Finally, I thank migrants everywhere who are helping us learn to love.

Rev. Dr. Steve Taylor
Director AngelWings Ltd, Senior Lecturer Flinders University
Maundy Thursday, 2024

Preface

This book grew out of my experiences working among, and being a member of, diaspora communities in several countries. I have participated in numerous missional initiatives, many run by congregations seeking to provide a service through which love might be expressed. Over my years of engagement, I began to wonder how we were doing: What were the aims of these initiatives, and did we know how to fulfill them? Were our initiatives an attempt to draw people into the church through the provision of a service in order to then preach the need for repentance, or were we simply aiming to provide nurture? Many church-based initiatives are intercultural, and I wondered if love was expressed in appropriate and meaningful ways across language and cultural barriers.

These experiences inspired me with the research question addressed in this book, "How is love of God and neighbor expressed at church-based, intercultural initiatives, and what might help this?" These questions gave shape to my PhD research and in turn resulted in this book. What I found surprised me at times. Long and faithful service was offered by many people I observed at the four initiatives I studied in the city of Melbourne. Despite this, the aims of the initiatives were not always clear, and time to pray, plan, and reflect was not easy to come by. For better or worse, participants were the sum of their past formation, which motivated and fueled their service. This past formation included varying levels of intercultural competence. I sought to discover what spiritual and practical formation was required for successful demonstrations of love.

Based on this study, this book seeks to offer much needed guidance on relational mission. I discovered that the principles and practices of pastoral care enable us to love others well, and in so doing we express love of God and neighbor. These principles and practices are largely applicable to any missions context and emphasize the importance of fostering pastoral care

PREFACE

skills, practical skills, spiritual formation, and reflective practice. Church-based initiatives do not function in isolation from the rest of church life. Core church narratives, teachings, and other aspects of church life all impact what takes place during sessions. I suggest ways the principles and practices of pastoral care may be harnessed to improve the quality of service offered to people who attend.

I introduce pastoral care themes in relation to mission in this book. It is my hope that further research will take place, building on what I have written here and enriching our understanding of the concepts introduced. May we learn to love others well—with respect, mutuality, and spiritual nurture.

SUE M. HOLDSWORTH
April 2024

Acknowledgments

THIS BOOK IS THE result of several community efforts. I have many people to thank: Participants and pastors at the four congregations I studied invited me into their lives and thoughts, for which I thank them. Rev. Dr. Alan Niven, my PhD supervisor at the University of Divinity, went well beyond expectations in reviewing and editing my thesis, and Dr. Brian Macallan's missiological reflections were valuable in shaping my work. Rev. Prof. Glen O'Brien dedicated many hours to reading and commenting on a draft of this book. Rev. Dr. Steve Taylor has provided valuable mentoring and graciously agreed to write the foreword. Thank you to all my friends who enabled this project financially. Your generosity is noted with love and gratitude. Finally, I wish to thank Julian for standing by while I worked, offering encouragement and technical support.

PART 1

1

Introduction

MISSIOLOGISTS GENERALLY AGREE THAT the local church has, rightly, become the locus of mission.[1] Globalization and the refugee crisis have arrived on the doorstep of Western nations, who are now more in need of mission than many of the traditional receiving nations. The Western church is in catastrophic decline, but committed, church-based volunteers are still to be found, seeking to meet local needs at church-based initiatives.

The thesis of this book is that effective mission takes place when we engage in pastoral care. When we proclaim God's love through our actions, Christianity becomes attractive. When asked what the greatest commandment is, Jesus replied, "'Love the Lord your God with all your heart and with all your soul and with all your mind and with all your strength.' The second is this: 'Love your neighbor as yourself'" (Mark 12:30–31). This describes the essence of pastoral care.

This book will explore ways in which church-based volunteers can strengthen their expressions of love of God and neighbor through implementing practices of pastoral care. It is based on my PhD study of four church-based initiatives in the city of Melbourne, Australia. My findings have relevance to a much wider audience including students, academics, pastors, and mission workers in any nation. I argue that instead of framing our volunteering at church-based initiatives as mission, we should view them as pastoral care. I define pastoral care as the complex discipline it is and illustrate how its functions align closely with mission in a way that

1. Kim and Fitchett-Climenhaga, "Introduction to Mission Studies."

PART 1

respects and celebrates others and invites them to set the pace and depth of relationships.

I note how pastoral care practices might have aided mission at the locations studied and make helpful suggestions for other, similar church-based initiatives. An overt link between the practice of the disciplines of mission and pastoral care has not previously been clearly established from the study of on-the-ground projects. This book seeks to remedy this by directly exploring applied foundational practices of pastoral care in the context of mission practice. I suggest an approach to mission that requires self-understanding and frequent reflection. This approach is subversive in its humility, requiring a disposition that resists telling others what to do but instead seeks to invite the other to direct our interactions and to change ourselves through them. Mission scholars regularly write of the importance of spirituality for mission. I will demonstrate how a pastoral care model (which includes spiritual formation of volunteers) helps volunteers grow spiritually through reflection on their service. I demonstrate a link between the core narratives of each setting and what took place at the initiatives, thus confirming that the formation of core narratives in congregational life will be reflected in the "how and why" of church initiatives. This book also explores the extent to which the operational theologies of volunteers were formed by core narratives and how some volunteers thought and practiced independently. I compare three volunteer situations with one professional situation. This allows one mode of service to speak to the other. The contrast between volunteer and professional roles highlights an important dimension of service in the local church setting.

Perhaps our strong tendency to silo academic disciplines has hidden this approach in plain sight. Maybe we have not considered it, believing pastoral care to be only about care in crisis or having cups of tea with the elderly, important as those things are. Pastoral care teaches us to love well, a vital component of mission. It is a more complex discipline than many of us have realized, yet the dispositions of heart necessary for effective pastoral care can guide us as we seek to discern how God would have us respond to others.

Modern Australia, like Canada, New Zealand, and the United States, was built on successive waves of migrants.[2] Europe has experienced growing rates of migration in recent decades, and the refugee crisis is being experienced in most nations worldwide. Many people reading this book

---

2. I note here that modern Australia was built on the unceded lands of the First Nations peoples.

will be descended from migrants, be a migrant (as I am), or have migrant friends and acquaintances. Melbourne, where my research was conducted, is one city among many in the world where the church has sought to welcome migrants by offering services, such as English conversation classes, to help them settle in a new country.

Many refugees and asylum seekers have specialist needs, due to backgrounds of trauma and waiting for many years to be settled in another country. In addition to the loss of friends and family, migration often results in limited work and disrupted education.[3] Refugees and asylum seekers often suffer the ongoing effects of trauma, indicating a clear need for therapeutic or pastoral support. Adapting to a new society is challenging for migrants with little or no ability in the language of their new home country. A five-year longitudinal study of humanitarian migrants explored the prevalence of mental illness among this cohort, finding strong links between severe mental health problems and post-migration difficulties among refugees.[4]

Although trauma has often negatively affected migrants, the difficulties faced in their new country are of greater significance in predicting long-term mental health outcomes.[5] Congregations and organizations have sought to help settle new migrants in Melbourne since the mid-twentieth century. Intercultural initiatives are often organically initiated within congregations in response to a perceived need, ranging from a grandparent program in which children from migrant families are "adopted" by surrogate grandparents, to regular day outings for asylum seekers. The use of conversational English during activities such as cooking enables migrants to practice English, make friends, and learn and teach new skills. I remember working among young Asians who were being exploited by landlords in Melbourne. In response, a Presbyterian church established two accommodation houses at a fair rent. Denominationally based social services offer advocacy and daily support for asylum seekers.[6] Despite being a nation built upon migration, federal government analysis indicates that few Australians appear to have a comprehensive understanding of the depth and extent of cultural differences.[7] Intercultural relating (or introductory

---

3. Achren et al., *Responding to CALD Learners*.
4. National Centre for Longitudinal Data, *Building a New Life in Australia*.
5. Schweitzer et al., "Mental Health," 1–9.
6. "Multicultural Services."
7. Federation of Ethnic Communities' Council of Australia, *Cultural Competence in Australia*.

PART 1

anthropology) is not taught in schools, although more recently the value of tolerance (to be distinguished from acceptance and embrace) towards those who are different is taught.[8]

Awareness of migrant social needs has grown in churches, and, in response, the Baptist Union of Victoria appointed a dedicated, part-time pastor to assist migrant congregations or congregations with high migrant contact.[9] Other denominations have similar roles, and some large congregations have a pastor for multicultural ministries. Churches rely heavily on volunteers to conduct community programs such as language classes, which presents a challenge when standards of teaching and the qualifications of the (mostly) volunteer teachers for these English classes vary. These classes are popular among migrants who often attend in addition to the government-allocated 510 hours of lessons. Many are searching for a place of community and belonging. The four churches in this book developed their projects and teams against this historical backdrop of variously motivated missions and services to migrants and refugees. Can these four initiatives be read as a narrative of seventy-five years of mission or seventy-five years of pastoral care, and how have these diverse models been reflected in current practice? This book explores where the differences may lie.

My own experiences of being a British migrant in France, time spent training in the United States, migrating as a family to South Korea, and then to Australia, have taught me some of the challenges faced by migrants. I have experienced welcome and also indifference, even hostility. I have been welcomed empathetically by other migrants, who taught me how to live in South Korea. This welcome was followed by our arrival in Australia, to a community that failed to understand the strangeness of everyday life in a country that felt so different, even though we spoke the same language. Our first family Christmas in Australia was a lonely experience in contrast to those we spent with the expat community in Seoul, which was very hospitable to new arrivals. The South African community in our church cared for one another, as did the Cantonese congregation, but the local Australians did not understand our new-migrant needs or the common experiences of dislocation. However, both the South African and the Cantonese communities warmly welcomed my intentional interactions.

Once established in Melbourne, I sought out opportunities to extend welcome to new migrants. This included making friends in the Cantonese

8. "Multicultural Education Programs and Resources."
9. "Resources."

congregation at church and volunteering at language classes and at a youth group for young East Asian students. The study of anthropology and mission opened my eyes to the wisdom of all cultures and helped me come to terms with my own migration experiences. Over time, my membership with three international missions helped me explore interculturality. In my most recent role, I helped a number of churches relate interculturally among each other and in their local community. My study of four church-based initiatives taught me that loving others well, through practices of pastoral care, results in emotionally nonviolent mission in which care is offered on the other's terms.

My PhD research was inspired by my work with a mission agency where my role was to help churches relate interculturally, both within the church and in their local community. Although the pastors of these churches verbally endorsed my strategy of several weeks of observations and consultations within the congregation, my suggestions were often resisted. My desire to develop evidence-informed research grew stronger. Concurrently I set up an intercultural initiative in a very multicultural, multireligious suburb, where many newly arrived asylum seekers lived. It seemed that local churches had little interaction with these communities, so my initiative to asylum seekers sought the involvement of local congregations. I thought that they would be more inclined to participate in a project initiated by someone from outside their communities, which proved to be correct. I was joined by members from local churches, two pastors, and workers from two other mission organizations representing a diverse range of missional outlooks and goals.

I intended the project to be a welcoming "safe place" for asylum seekers to meet one another and other local residents, with options for learning English. Another missions worker believed we should filter *everyone* into English classes and worked hard to achieve this. Both local pastors believed we should preach the gospel to asylum seekers at every opportunity. One pastor wanted to demonstrate to the local council that Christians were involved with asylum seekers and would often invite local and national media to attend. This sometimes confused, ambivalent, and diverse blend of roles, aims, and project designs seemed to characterize local church endeavors. This scenario formed one of the foundations for my research and also identified the core issue of motivations.

I challenged the strong push for English lessons *for all*, the style of evangelism, and the frequent, invited presence of the media. These aspects of the church's endeavors seemed to pressure and manipulate a group of mostly traumatized asylum seekers who basically needed to feel safe and genuinely welcomed. My suggestion of a joint memorandum of understanding was resisted. I withdrew, unable to align with such approaches and more motivated than ever towards my original, embryonic question, "What really happens when congregations engage in intercultural outreach programs?"

I have been the lone foreigner in a strange land, participating in forming a ghetto of foreigners set apart from their hosts, which reinforces shared prejudices and misconceptions. I have been a part of a group who viewed new immigrants as targets for evangelism, while offering services that we had decided they most needed. I too have sometimes been ethnocentric and patronizing in my cross-cultural interactions. I have learned, however, that mutually rewarding friendships can be formed cross-culturally and across religious differences.

The contribution of church-based volunteers to the integration of migrant communities into society is significant in its social service provision. However, volunteers may be untrained or poorly supervised and this can result in a poor quality of service and even psychological harm to clients. While church-based groups meet various needs of local communities, personal experience suggests that there is often a lack of group focus and formation, community consultation, or clarity of goals. With little to no training or ongoing assessment and perhaps a manipulative process of loving others with the undeclared motivation of gaining converts, service of others can easily be compromised. Some parts of the church may assume that any activity engaged in by members within the community should be missional, although they may differ in what they mean by this. Members might desire to see conversions, and this is often assumed to be the ultimate *raison d'être* of church-based initiatives. This can result in conflicting aims and the provision of services may develop as thinly disguised excuses for gospel proclamation. Other volunteers may believe that initiatives should exist simply to communicate care. These two poles of tension within church-based, intercultural initiatives may find clearer articulation through the theological principles and practices of intercultural pastoral care rather than in describing them as mission.

Given this complex set of motivations, aims, and practices, more needs to be understood about the inherent dynamics of such initiatives. It is necessary to understand the practices, motivations, and skill levels of volunteers in order to bring recommendations for enhancing the ability of volunteers to express love of God and neighbor. This book is an exploration of formation for volunteering, with a focus on church-based and intercultural initiatives. Because it is church-based, this study is rooted in church narratives and therefore explores how corporate messaging or influence is reflected in individual behaviors. Individuals' theologies affect actions in social engagement and invite discovery of how one might achieve a deeper level of spiritual formation.

All paid and volunteer personnel engaged in church-based activities need some form of ongoing reflective practice, ethical awareness, and professional development. Reflective practice as the basis for effective pastoral care and mission is generally supported through appropriate combinations of one-on-one supervision, group supervision, and self-awareness. Consequently, the allied disciplines of Clinical Pastoral Education (CPE), reflective practice, and intercultural competence are considered here. Discerning motivation for service and development of integrative skills relies on processes firmly anchored in theological reflection.

INTRODUCING THE FOUR CONGREGATIONS

This book discusses volunteers and paid staff (jointly referred to as participants) from four quite different congregations in different denominations and socioeconomic areas of Melbourne. Many of the features of these settings might be found in similar cities around the world. They are all evangelical congregations, although much of what I write is expected to be relevant to anyone seeking to extend love to people outside the church. All participants volunteered to take part in this research project. When referring generally to all participants, I will, at times, refer to them all as volunteers, even though these "volunteers" were paid staff at Northern Training.

Swindon Baptist is a large congregation in a wealthy, multicultural suburb.[10] It offers services in several languages other than English and is concerned to be a place of welcome for the local community. To this end, it offers English conversation classes to new migrants on most days of the week. I became a participant observer at the Tuesday morning classes, an involvement which lasted around five months. I interviewed each of the nine participant volunteers and attended services and other church events to get a feel for the congregation.

10. Names, locations, and other identifying features of churches have been anonymized.

PART 1

Digswell Anglican is a large, multi-congregational church in the western suburbs of Melbourne. They had been running a sewing club for refugee women on a social housing estate for twelve years when I joined them. The four participant volunteers were very concerned to see converts, and this was apparent in their conversations with me, for example, when they spoke of "opportunities" to share the gospel. The club was attended by Muslim refugee women who might have been persecuted by their community if they converted to Christianity. In all their years of service, the team were unaware of any converts. This deeply discouraged them, and the people they served were described as "difficult." I was told they ministered on "tough ground."

Govan Church of Christ is a congregation with around sixty members. It is in a northern suburb, an area where many migrants settle. English conversation classes ran on Saturday mornings and had started in response to need. The group leader ran the classes in an experienced and thoughtful manner. Although the atmosphere at classes was friendly and welcoming, no group prayer or planning took place, and I had the impression of a group of individual volunteers coexisting a space each week.

Hope International Church is different to the other locations, as study participants in the provision of childcare services for migrants were paid. Hope International is a very large Pentecostal church, also located in the northern suburbs. Church leaders wanted their church to be good news in the local area and undertook market research to discover local needs they might help meet. They discovered that many migrant women had come to the area knowing no one and that their qualifications were not recognized in Australia. Childcare was under provided for locally, so the church took the step of opening a government-accredited training school to train child day care educators, Northern Training. This offered new migrants the opportunity for training for employment and a means of integrating into society. Most teachers at the school were from the congregation, themselves migrants, and had retrained as child day care educators. This project had also started in response to need, although study participants were waged. Most told me they could have earned higher wages in other jobs but were willing to sacrifice wages for a shared sense of ministry.

INTRODUCTION

DEFINING PASTORAL CARE

Pastoral care offers a spiritual presence that steps gently into the narrative world of another, a process that can be understood as hospitality given, received, and mutually shared.[11] Pastoral care pays attention to the message of God's love, the people who are communicating the message, and the context in which this message is communicated. This statement carries formational and motivational implications for practitioners. Pastoral care seeks to help relatively healthy people develop strengths to fulfill their hopes and potential.[12]

The functions of pastoral care are healing, sustaining, guiding, reconciling, nurturing, liberating (including advocacy), and empowering.[13] They sit comfortably within an understanding of mission viewed as participation in the *missio Dei*. Literally meaning God's mission, this is the concept that all mission originates in the sending relationships within the Trinity. God's mission is to draw all creation to himself, empowering us to live in relationship with him.

Jesus healed the sick (Luke 18:35–43); fed hungry crowds (Matt 14:13–21); he taught and guided people, as when he spoke to Mary and Martha (Luke 10:38–42); and his death and resurrection opened the path to reconciliation with God (Matt 27:32—28:6). His demonstrations of forgiveness are ultimate examples of liberating reconciliation (John 8:1–11). Children were nurtured when Jesus invited them to gather around (Mark 10:13–16), and he was himself nurtured through his relationship with God the Father (Matt 14:23). The parable of the good Samaritan (Luke 10:25–37) and the story of Mary Magdalene washing Jesus' feet (John 12:1–8) enact liberation by cutting through racial and social prejudice. Jesus surrendered his power through the act of incarnation (Luke 2:29–32; Phil 2:1–11) to empower all humanity. The life and ministry of Jesus prophetically signposted how his followers were to live (e.g., Matt 5–7). He embodied the functions of pastoral care in his mission, reminding us that the mission of all believers is to love as Jesus was loved by God. These functions are not new to Christians engaged in mission. The church has a two-millennia-old record of healing through medical care, counseling,

---

11. Doehring, *Practice of Pastoral Care*, xxii.
12. Clinebell and McKeever, *Basic Types of Pastoral Care*, 26.
13. Lartey, *In Living Color*, 63–69. Lartey builds on the work of Clebsch and Jaekle, *Pastoral Care in Historical Perspective*, 4, and Clinebell and McKeever, *Basic Types of Pastoral Care*, 41.

providing food relief, advocating for those with no voice, helping others live improved lives, and calling out injustice.

Intercultural pastoral care has additional dimensions. Western paradigms of care are not necessarily helpful in intercultural care settings.[14] For instance, the individualism prevalent in Western cultures is not helpful as a basis for care in cultures in which individuals are viewed as one of a group. A deep respect for difference is important in the provision of intercultural pastoral care, which builds trust as carers respect the different practices, values, and religious beliefs of care receivers.[15] Learning about differences in worldview, and the provision by church leaders of educational and formational tools for recognizing and overcoming ethnocentric tendencies, is important for the Christian practice of pastoral care.

Spiritual Formation for Pastoral Care

As pastoral care is a function of the church, the spiritual formation of caregivers is necessary for mature, reasoned, compassionate demonstrations of God's love. Pastoral theology enables this and, so, should guide practice and reflection. "Habitus" is important for pastoral carers. This refers to reflexive actions that become second nature, arising from long standing practice.[16]

Nurturing relationships with God, self, and others is an essential characteristic of participant spirituality. It is out of these nurtured relationships that individuals can effectively express God's love.[17] These three dimensions of participant spirituality became significant factors as the volunteers and activities at the four sites began to reveal their meaning. How we love others relates to how we love ourselves, and we become fully ourselves through our exchanges with others.[18] The move from self-love to building community, and then to mutuality in care, is firmly anchored in one's spirituality for mission or for pastoral care. Mutuality is expressed when a missionary (or caregiver) receives back from others.[19] How does this sit with mission? Moving from a mindset that places us at the center of what God is doing

---

14. Lartey, *In Living Color*, 110.
15. Doehring, *Practice of Pastoral Care*, 1.
16. Ballard and Pritchard, *Practical Theology in Action*, 177.
17. Nouwen, *Reaching Out*.
18. Benner, *Desiring God's Will*, 103.
19. Gittins, *Gifts and Strangers*, 105.

INTRODUCTION

enables us to move into a church life rooted in the *missio Dei*.[20] The journey of nurturing love to and from God, ourselves, and others will, therefore, be an important factor in discerning whether the care offered by volunteers reflects the life-bringing essence of God.

Interpathy is also important for pastoral care. Interpathy occurs when a caregiver brackets out their own beliefs to step into the mind of and respect the worldview of a care seeker. It is a necessary skill for intercultural care.[21] Interpathy supports the provision of sensitive intercultural mission, where those on mission listen and respond to others within their values, perspectives, and priorities. This is a respectful way of avoiding colonization or cultural misinterpretation of needs. *The Cape Town Commitment* of the Lausanne Movement (a movement that consists of mostly evangelical Protestants) calls for mission to be rooted in love,[22] and the apostolic exhortation *Evangelii Gaudium* describes empathy as "touching the suffering flesh of Christ in others."[23] Embodied, incarnational expressions of empathy and interpathy are the indicators of both effective mission and authentic pastoral care.

Self-evidently, intercultural competence undergirds the service of church-based volunteers at intercultural initiatives. Numerous models of intercultural competence exist. Of these, the Cultural Intelligence (CQ) model has been modified and applied to mission.[24] Another important value that merits consideration for pastoral care is Kluckhohn and Murray's theory of humanness, which states,

> Every man is in certain respects
> a. like all other men,
> b. like some other men,
> c. like no other man.[25]

Spiritual formation that expresses this inclusive, respectful sensitivity sits alongside the development of intercultural competence to enable these skills to be expressed as the love of God for each unique individual.

---

20. Roxburgh and Boren, *Introducing the Missional Church*, 69–70.
21. Augsburger, *Pastoral Counseling*, 27–32.
22. *Cape Town Commitment*.
23. Francis, *Evangelii Gaudium*, sec. 24.
24. Livermore, *Cultural Intelligence*.
25. Kluckhohn and Murray, "Personality in Nature," 35, quoted in Augsburger, *Pastoral Counseling*, 49.

PART 1

Supervision and Reflective Practice

Professional supervision that supports reflective practice is recommended for all pastoral workers and anyone in a church-based caring role. This has long applied across all caring disciplines as best practice and is akin to the pastoral cycle in which practice informs reflection and new insights are in turn applied to practice. The pastoral cycle has also been termed the "praxis model" for mission in liberation theology.[26] The Theological Action Research (TAR) model is a collaborative and integrative model, designed for use in church-based contexts, where groups reflect theologically on what has taken place in the context of church ministry to achieve best practice.[27] The main purpose of these models is to enable practitioners, professional or volunteer, to gain self-awareness, challenge unhelpful beliefs and behaviors, and, therefore, improve practice. All opportunities for supervision (formal/informal, group/individual, professional/peer) undergird understanding of practice and provide windows into the motivation and meaning of each missional activity.

DEFINING MISSION

Defining mission has been a task for numerous missiologists with some even questioning whether we should abandon the term, as it has come to mean quite different things to different people.[28] My definition of mission for the purposes of this book is based on Bevans's theology of mission for the twenty-first century,[29] which builds on twentieth-century definitions, notably those of Bosch.[30] I will weave his understanding into my own commentary to ground the discussion of mission as pastoral care.

The concept of the *missio Dei*, which proposes that mission is sourced in the trinitarian relationships, became central to mission theology by the late twentieth century.[31] The role of Christians is to discern where the Spirit is already at work and to join in. This concept rightly removes Christians and the church from the center of mission.

---

26. Bevans, *Models of Contextual Theology*, 63–80.
27. Cameron et al., *Talking about God in Practice*.
28. Stroope, *Transcending Mission*.
29. Bevans, "Theologies of Mission."
30. Bosch, *Transforming Mission*.
31. Bosch, *Transforming Mission*, 389–93; Flett, *Witness of God*, ch. 1.

A shift in focus regarding mission in the twenty-first century is now discernible, as suggested by Bevans, who suggests that mission today needs to be understood as "prophetic dialogue," as "transforming/missionary discipleship," and as a "missiology of attraction."[32] These categories fit well with an understanding of mission as pastoral care.

Mission as Prophetic Dialogue

Christians speak or act prophetically in all aspects of society, from government to private life. This should be done through gentle, ongoing dialogue.[33] This is not to imply that Christians should always be speaking against things but rather that they should be speaking up for the rights of the oppressed, the marginalized, and the poor. This includes bringing hope and peace in situations of despair. Note here the term "dialogue." We do not preach to the non-Christian world in a manner that sees Christianity at the center of society. Instead, we dialogue in an exchange of viewpoints and outlooks with quiet but firm assurance that relationship with God is lifegiving and, therefore, liberating. Such dialogue takes place within friendships in a context of hospitality, a common theme in the pastoral care literature. This includes interfaith dialogue that respects and learns from the other.

Many in the West have been turned off by Christianity because Christians have too often communicated that they have all the answers. Rather, we are to listen to and learn from others. We avoid reducing people to targets as we live among them, engaging in the many exchanges this brings.[34]

Prophetic mission takes place through actions as well as words. The life of the Christian community as a whole, and not only the life of individual Christians, speaks powerfully of the love of God. The love, compassion, and forgiveness experienced within Christian community is to be offered as a gift to those outside the church. This is a powerful expression of God's love through which the gospel message is communicated by way of invitation into the life of God and the church.[35]

Congregations engage in prophetic dialogue through loving action when they care for their community. In addition to these prophetic actions demonstrating love of God and neighbor, journeying alongside people of

---

32. Bevans, "Theologies of Mission," 111–28.
33. Bevans, "Theologies of Mission."
34. Bevans, "Theologies of Mission."
35. Jones, *Evangelistic Love of God*.

PART 1

other faiths or no faith creates opportunities for verbal dialogue, as both parties listen to each other and speak of what is important to them. Conducting missional activities does not guarantee this dialogue and it should not be forced, but they create contexts in which verbal exchanges may happen. As Bevans stresses, this is not an opportunity for evangelistic persuasion; rather, it provides opportunity for genuine dialogue.[36]

Transforming/Missionary Discipleship

Christian disciples are to be connected to Christ in an ongoing manner that is expressed as mission. This connection is nurtured by ongoing spiritual practices including prayer, reflection, and discernment—all pastoral themes. As believers become more Christlike, God's missionary purposes will be fulfilled.

This requires us to engage in discipleship that transforms us and the world around us. This extends the concept of the identity of the church as missional. Discipleship of believers is ongoing, not a once-and-for-all decision to convert to Christ. This ongoing process involves several practices common to pastoral care, including prayer and spiritual reflection. Discipleship also includes standing in solidarity with people on the margins, another pastoral care practice.[37] Mission requires discipleship that stays connected to God so that his missionary purposes are furthered in all aspects of life.

Mission as Attraction

Mission happens when, through pastoral care, Christian living becomes attractive to others. When practices of care, community, hospitality, respect, and connection are present and rooted in practices of connectedness to God, people are more likely to become interested in the Christian life. This is what it means for our "light to shine before others" (Matt 5:16). Where love, joy, welcome, forgiveness, and equality are present, God's love for humanity is reflected and becomes inherently attractive.

Mission as attraction is a powerful antidote to a view of Christians in the public sphere as demanding and unloving. It counters the presentation

---

36. Bevans, "Theologies of Mission," 111–28.
37. Bevans, "Theologies of Mission."

of Christianity as a set of propositions, replacing it with a dynamic encounter of love and acceptance.

COMPLEMENTARY DISCIPLINES: THEMES OF PASTORAL CARE AND MISSION

Pastoral care and missiology are complementary disciplines. Pastoral care practices prevent mission from becoming preoccupied with conversion and cultural hegemony.[38] When pastoral care and mission are merged, we engage more authentically in the practice of holistic care. When people are empowered to live healthy lives, the gospel becomes good news.[39] The goals of mission, community engagement and community building, and pastoral care are also merged by missional church writers who describe caring for others as the mission to which the church is called, thus reframing mission to include pastoral care.[40] Merging, or enabling dialogue between these two disciplines—while no simple task—can unlock potential for interpretation of activities at the four initiatives, enabling deeper encounters where, rather than being a target for gospel proclamation, others are considered potential friends with whom to journey and in whom to encourage growth.

Church-based community initiatives often display confusion about the relationship between pastoral care and mission. While I usually found that neither had been discussed among volunteers, I discovered that motivations tended towards wanting to provide pastoral care to migrants through the provision of a service, rather than mission in the sense of making converts. They offered care as part of God's mission of reconciliation to the extent that they nurtured spirituality through prayer and discernment. This is pastoral care functioning as mission.

Pastoral care requires acts of listening, discerning, reflection, prayer, self-awareness, and supervision. Where Christian groups are engaged in caring initiatives, these must become group practices, or the transforming power of loving, God-centered community cannot be experienced. Pastoral care creates a context for proclamation. Many people will respond with indifference to reasoned propositions about Christian belief. Christianity needs to be experienced. Proclamation needs to be culturally sensitive, especially in the post-Christendom West. Pastoral care can create

38. Pattison, "Is Pastoral Care Dead?," 7–10.
39. Sims, "Response to Stephen Pattison," 285–86.
40. Roxburgh, *Joining God*, 8; Frost, *Exiles*, 126.

the potential for such sensitive proclamation if it is invited by those with whom we are in relationship. If this potential is not realized, we are called to keep on loving and enjoying the company of one another. People should not be our projects, and we make idols of ourselves if we think we are the only person who might bring a person to Christ. We are called to keep loving, learning from, and receiving the good gifts that others bring into our lives. God's plans for those outside the church are far bigger than our role. The reflective practice engaged in by pastoral carers is not prescriptive and encourages ongoing assessment of effective practices and identification of what seems problematic. The spiritually based reflective practices that serve as a basis for the practice of pastoral care should be insisted upon for anyone engaged in mission.

During times of persecution in the early church, public preaching was not always a viable option, yet it grew phenomenally through acts of care and hospitality.[41] While Christians are not persecuted in the West, we would do well to follow their model as we practice our faith in a sometimes verbally hostile environment. Acts of care break through this hostility to model the reign of Christ.

The practices of mission and pastoral care meet in their offer of transformative love. Motivations for providing pastoral care and engaging in mission are different, however, when the primary aim of mission is evangelism. As a primary motivation, evangelism can easily undermine pastoral care. These modalities merge when the aim of pastoral care is to express love in whatever manner is appropriate.

SUMMARY AND CHAPTER OUTLINE

Many churches have a rich history of sustaining and nurturing migrants. My own journey notes mistakes as well as points of effectiveness in demonstrating love of God and neighbor. God's people are called to care for the stranger, and to do this effectively requires embodied principles of pastoral care—essentially a mission rooted in the *missio Dei*. Reflective practice and supervision are means by which such care can be sustained and enhanced. This book explores how four church-based, intercultural initiatives in Melbourne exercised care through community service and offers recommendations for evidence-informed practice. The disciplines of pastoral care,

---

41. Kreider, *Patient Ferment of the Early Church*.

mission, spiritual formation, and ministry supervision will be explored as a pathway towards best practice.

Chapter 2 describes how and why I used certain research methods. Although some may prefer to skim over this chapter, other readers will find it necessary as a demonstration of the reliability of my work and my method of data collection and analysis. In chapter 3 I introduce three biblical passages that root this study and link them to major themes from my findings. Chapter 4 describes in detail the missional activities at the four locations studied. Chapter 5 is a short chapter that summarizes major findings. This sets the scene for part 2 in which the information offered so far is discussed. Chapter 6 relates findings to the functions of pastoral care, while chapter 7 explores expressions of love noted at the initiatives and discusses what might have strengthened these. Chapter 8 concerns motivations for service, observed through observations and triangulated through interviewing the volunteers. Chapter 9 is about skills needed for both intercultural relating and for delivery of the services offered at the initiatives. The final chapter draws together the previous chapters and makes recommendations for group and individual formation for volunteers (and anyone involved in mission) at church-based, intercultural initiatives.

Each chapter ends with questions for reflection and discussion. These are aimed to help pastors and church-based volunteers integrate the teaching in this book with their own church-based, intercultural initiatives. Many questions will also be helpful for other readers (e.g., scholars, students, and cross-cultural missionaries) grounding book learning in real life situations.

QUESTIONS FOR REFLECTION AND DISCUSSION

- To what extent have I viewed mission and pastoral care as separate disciplines?
- How might I merge my understanding of mission and pastoral care at our church-based, intercultural initiative or in my interactions with people outside the church?

2

Researching Practice

There were men in the community room that the sewing club women were waiting to use. The room was booked for the club, so the men shouldn't have been there. But who was going to ask them to leave? The community was Muslim, and it wasn't appropriate for a woman to approach them. Fortunately, Dave, the pastor, was nearby. He politely pointed out to the men that the room was already booked for the club. The men were apologetic, quickly put their chairs away, and left. No offence was caused thanks to volunteers who understood a little of the men's culture.

THE FOUR RESEARCH LOCATIONS: FOUR CONGREGATIONS

Swindon Baptist Church is in an affluent Melbourne suburb with many wealthy migrants. One morning each week, for fourteen weeks, English conversation classes were observed.[1] This was one of several classes run throughout the week to serve the English language needs of the local migrant residents. Classes ran from 10:00 until 11:30 a.m., and usually one of the volunteers opened with a talk of general interest, such as places to visit near Melbourne. Students were then allocated to different volunteer tutors. Some tutors had the same students each week; others had different students. Most classes had up to four students, although one beginner's class

---

1. Visits were made between March and June 2015.

RESEARCHING PRACTICE

was considerably larger. A suite of classrooms surrounded a central café. Swindon Baptist had six congregations at the time of the study. Three were English speaking. In addition, there was a Mandarin-speaking congregation, a Cantonese-speaking congregation, and a Nigerian congregation that spoke Yoruba. The membership could be described as broadly evangelical.

Interviews took place over several weeks, immediately following classes. I met initially with potential participants to explain my research, attended nine church services, one tutors' social event, one newcomers' event, and three English teaching training sessions. Nine volunteers participated and three of the pastoral staff were interviewed, plus the class founder. Most were practicing Christians, although this was less clear in the case of two volunteers. I attended a variety of other church events: a newcomers' welcome session, several Sunday services, and a meal out with the English class volunteers. This provided wider contextual, cultural, and theological data for the study.[2] All volunteers were in either early or mid-retirement and presented as reasonably affluent. Previous employment details and informal conversations about lifestyle suggested that most were financially secure. The English lessons were observed over five months.

The four congregations of Digswell Anglican met in diverse socioeconomic settings. The congregation for this study met in a common room on the ground floor of a high-rise block on a social housing estate and was attended by locals, all aged over fifty with identified social needs. Approximately twenty were Syrian asylum seekers and migrants. Several members of other Digswell congregations with some leadership capacity also attended. The sewing club followed the church service and was run in a different building on the estate. The club aimed to meet the needs of the many Muslim women on the estate, mostly Sudanese and Ethiopian refugees who had arrived in Australia around twenty years previously. The club had no formal membership and the women arrived and left as they pleased. Many hours of observation of club activities were followed by interviews where I learned that congregational volunteers had initiated and run the sewing club for local migrant women for many years. Volunteers ranged in age from twenty to early sixties, all highly educated, articulate, and well presented. The leader was a lawyer and had run the group for twelve years. I attended three church services, one community meal preceding the service, a planning meeting, and a post-camp debriefing for a family camp for

2. Patton, *Qualitative Research*, 69.

housing estate residents. Interviews were conducted with each sewing club volunteer, the pastor, and two volunteers who attended camp.

Govan Church of Christ was established in the 1970s. This church had around sixty attendees on Sunday mornings. Govan is a largely blue-collar suburb in Melbourne's north, and was originally a township separated from Melbourne's outer suburbs. Today the area is highly multicultural. Seventeen visits meant each participant was observed on at least three or four occasions. One church service was attended. Bulletins dating between 1998 and 2016 were examined. All but one of the volunteers were interviewed, a total of nine people. Classes had been running every Saturday morning during school terms for several years. Classes had commenced in response to need, which was recognized following a visit to the congregation by two newly arrived asylum seekers. All but one participant attended the church.

While clean and functional, the building appeared in need of an overhaul, suggesting that money was tight. The church office and two meeting rooms were in portable buildings connected to the main church by a short undercover passageway. Classes were held in the main sanctuary on Saturday mornings between 10:00 and 11:30 a.m. Chairs were removed to make space for three tables at which students sat for the duration, including for morning tea. Students did not have regular teachers because they mostly chose where to sit, attended irregularly, and because most teachers attended on a rostered basis. Between one and three classes took place concurrently. When two or more classes took place, visits of fifteen to twenty minutes were made with breaks for discrete note-taking in between. Volunteers who prepared refreshments or set up for the lessons were also observed and informal chats in the kitchen developed. A church service was observed, and additional data came from sampling past church bulletins that provided information about church events and pastoral concerns.

All were practicing Christians, and all but one attended the congregation. All were of retirement age apart from one woman in her early thirties. Some were highly educated; others appeared much less educated, but all appeared to be people willing to think through issues. Only three volunteers attended classes every week, with the others rotating in. All were Caucasian, either Australian born or long-term migrants from Europe.

The fourth study was conducted at Hope International Church. I conducted observations and interviews from early October until mid-December 2017. I attended one graduation service. I interviewed all participants, the pastor with oversight of Northern Training, and the multicultural pastor, a total of eight interviews. As lessons took place six days a week during school terms, I conducted fieldwork in a shorter time frame and more intensively than in previous locations. I made seventeen visits.

I attended services at three different congregations of Hope International (the parent church of Northern Training). The area is a mix of blue-collar and recent immigrants, many from the Indian subcontinent. Hope International self-described as a Spirit-led church, focused on being real with each other, being generous, and being rooted in the Bible.

The church celebrated its fiftieth anniversary during my engagement with it. It held three English services on its main campus and two additional satellite services nearby. The pastor for multicultural ministries holds Saturday evening services for migrants from different world regions. These take place once a month for each region and, though still mainly in English, incorporate styles of worship and songs in a dominant regional language, such as Hindi.

A strong hierarchy was evident in the church, although the training school manager spoke of the senior pastor's vision as being owned by the whole church. While high levels of creativity were evident both in the training school and in church life in general (e.g., a use of drama and creative worship), only the senior pastors, plus one visiting speaker, were ever referred to as having received vision from God for the church.

The Registered Training Organization (RTO), Northern Training, was established and overseen by church leaders. Many of the local migrant population needed to retrain for work in Australia, and market research, conducted by church members, indicated that childcare was a booming business locally. In response, church leaders decided to start an RTO teaching childcare to enable new migrants to obtain employment. Graduates were known as childcare educators and tutors were known as trainers. A certificate IV or a diploma were given to students.[3] Around twenty full-time and part-time staff were employed. One senior staff member noted that around half were Christians and most attended the church. One staff member was Catholic and one was Orthodox. Other staff members represented several different religions. In addition to the Catholic and Orthodox trainers, one participant was Sikh and, although not part of the study, another staff member was Muslim. The RTO was housed upstairs in a large

---

3. A certificate IV and diplomas are offered in Australia at a tertiary level of education below undergraduate study.

shed-like building, adjacent to the large and very modern church. Two classes ran concurrently on Wednesdays and Saturdays.

Students were mostly young women from the Indian subcontinent, as were most staff. One participant had previously worked in the finance sector of a multinational company; one had been an engineer, and one a lawyer. The trainers (teachers) had retrained in childcare upon arriving in Australia, as a means of earning an income. Four participants stated that they were earning less by working at the RTO than they could elsewhere, but they would not consider leaving because they were happy and believed that God wanted them there. All participants indicated that they were very happy in this situation.

Once permission to study was granted by the pastors, the RTO manager talked privately to staff about the study and promised to recruit participants. Although this approach to recruitment was less direct, participants joined enthusiastically, completing and returning the consent forms. This approach reflected the hierarchical style of leadership: enthusiastic staff members were willing to do whatever they were asked. This cohort was much younger than previous cohorts studied, perhaps in their late thirties or early forties, and the predominance of Indian migrants was in contrast to the other locations.

I usually sat at the back or to the side of lessons and only commented when invited. Trainers would often come up to me and chat while the students worked individually. The trainers did not meet formally during the observation period, although I was often aware that some met informally. A lot of laughter was heard during these times. At lunchtimes I stayed in the classroom with the students as there was no other obvious place to go. Trainers usually did administration during breaks.

COLLECTING AND ANALYZING DATA

Conducting research and comparing findings from each location required consistently using specific research methods. It was important for me to take time to assess which methods would be most helpful for providing the understanding I sought. The following sections outline how and why I chose the methods I used to gain an understanding of the ways in which love of God and neighbor was expressed at the four initiatives.

A practical theological methodology enabled an understanding of what happened during the four initiatives, which resulted in the need to make interdisciplinary connections.[4] Qualitative research methods were considered the most helpful for me to gain a deep understanding of the dynamics I observed at each initiative. This included making detailed observations, interviewing volunteers, document searches, and casual conversations with volunteers.

Initial findings at each location were compared *in situ* and overall findings from each location were constantly compared with subsequent locations. For example, at Swindon I discovered the volunteers seemed generally reluctant to talk about their Christian faith, although some spoke more freely during interviews. This contrasted with Digswell where volunteers spoke freely about faith in front of the women attending sewing club. Volunteers at Govan were similar in approach to those at Swindon, while the sense of God's immanence among the Christian trainers at Northern Training resulted in what I would describe as a "faith overspill" in their interaction with the students. Thus, theory was built and discussed and ultimately developed into the recommendations in the final chapter.

I sought and was granted permission to study at each location, and while I focused on making observations with as little intrusion as possible, I also offered occasional help with tasks, such as serving refreshments and putting out chairs. I answered questions during sessions but kept personal input minimal to avoid influencing the course of events.

In interviews I explored perceptions of and motivations for participants' work with the underlying question: How is love of God and neighbor communicated effectively in the context of intercultural, church-based initiatives? All participants were Australian citizens or permanent residents. All participants cooperated fully and willingly with the research.

Grounded Theory

I sought to understand how love of God and neighbor was expressed at the four initiatives and what might strengthen this. Rather than impose a theoretical model on my emerging data, I required a methodology that enabled important points of understanding to emerge. Grounded theory (GT) seeks to develop new theory by studying a research field, allowing analysis of the data collected to result in new, mid-range, substantive theory, generalizable to other, similar initiatives. This approach fit well with my desire to let the initiatives speak with their own voice rather than impose my own theories

---

4. Rooms and Ross, "Practical Theology and Missiology," 114.

and assumptions. Theory is developed iteratively in GT; developing theory that emerges from analysis of data is taken back to the field and further tested, the result of which is either to challenge or strengthen it. Since its inception by Glaser and Strauss in the 1960s,[5] GT has been variously defined by theorists and research practitioners. Glaser's approach (which differed from Strauss as the years progressed) is regarded as classic GT.[6] It is positivist in nature and supported by researchers including Judith Holton and Isabelle Walsh.[7] Juliet Corbin and Anselm Strauss developed GT by taking a positivist interactionist approach, while Kathy Charmaz further added a constructivist approach.[8]

Each participant brought their own meaning and interpretations to the initiatives. Each had their own understanding of what they did and of what took place during sessions. My research, therefore, moved towards Constructivist Grounded Theory, in line with the approach taken by Kathy Charmaz.[9] This approach extends Corbin and Strauss in their embrace of symbolic interactionism,[10] in which both actors and researchers attach their own meanings to phenomena. This resonates with my self-description as post-foundationalist. This is an approach to practical theology that states while Christianity must maintain core beliefs, all other beliefs are open to interpretation.[11] In responding reflexively to emerging themes, I was persuaded by Charmaz's argument that GT relies on reasoning and making inferences; indeed, I employed reasoning or making inferences from the earliest stages of analysis.[12] For instance, through the use of gerunds during open coding I interpreted what I observed.[13] Phrases such as "seeking to console a student" and "explaining Christian beliefs about alcohol" encouraged me to explore why these actions occurred.

GT is an abductive method, meaning it relies on reasoning and choosing the most likely explanation from the facts.[14] This encourages imagina-

5. Glaser and Strauss, *Discovery of Grounded Theory*.
6. Bryant and Charmaz, "Grounded Theory Research."
7. Holton and Walsh, *Classic Grounded Theory*.
8. Charmaz, *Constructing Grounded Theory*.
9. Charmaz, *Constructing Grounded Theory*, 239.
10. Corbin and Strauss, *Basics of Qualitative Research*, 10.
11. Macallan, *Postfoundationalist Reflections*.
12. Charmaz, *Constructing Grounded Theory*, 201.
13. See Strauss, *Qualitative Analysis*.
14. Charmaz, *Constructing Grounded Theory*, 201. The concept of abduction was

tion and intuition. An example of this happening was at Digswell, where volunteers often brought talk about God into casual conversations with the women at sewing club. It seemed the most obvious explanation for this was that they wanted the women to become Christians. This more creative approach to analysis allows the possibility of deeper insight into data with the use of intuitive leaps, provided these leaps are adequately backed up by additional data. In this case, I listened and asked questions during interviews at Digswell to gain further evidence for my hunches that the club was primarily for evangelistic purposes.

Both Charmaz's and Strauss and Corbin's approaches to GT are based in symbolic interactionism.[15] I am only able to research within my constructed reality based on my life experiences and reactions to these, albeit rigorously and reflexively named and analyzed. As outlined in chapter 1, my previous experiences included involvement in several church-based, intercultural initiatives, from which I had developed my understanding of the needs and opportunities presented by these and similar initiatives. For Corbin and Strauss, theory is temporal,[16] for truth changes over time and so might one's reality and responses.[17] For example, any theory developed from the four settings in this study is open to change, amendment, or adaptation as new insight or other cultural shifts become dominant.

My self-description as post-foundationalist complements a constructivist approach to analysis in GT. Knowledge is discernible through explanations of constructed realities. Corbin and Strauss suggest that knowledge may emerge from multiple constructions.[18] Critical analysis of four initiatives, where I sought to answer the research question when viewed from different perspectives, created new knowledge in the form of theory.

Constant Comparison of Data: An Iterative Approach to Grounded Theory

By constantly comparing data, analysis revealed that volunteer motivations varied, even within each initiative. While some volunteers sought to simply

---

introduced by the pragmatist Charles Sanders Peirce. See Peirce, *Collected Papers*.

15. Charmaz, *Constructing Grounded Theory*, 261–84.

16. Corbin and Strauss, *Basics of Qualitative Research*, 55.

17. For discussion of symbolic interactionism, see also Charmaz, *Constructing Grounded Theory*, 265–72.

18. Corbin and Strauss, *Basics of Qualitative Research*, 3.

offer a service during sessions, many others desired to care for attendees in other ways and at other times. This was made apparent during interviews and through interactions during sessions. Motivations for service at Govan were generally similar to those at Swindon, while differing from Digswell. I then compared possible reasons for these differences, finding at least a partial answer in the fact that three groups had not discussed the aims of the initiatives.

The fourth study at Northern Training acted as a contrast since the participants were employed. Emergent themes were, however, surprisingly like those at Swindon and Govan. Participants were motivated by care and empathy and had self-selected into the role, with those less willing to fit into the ethos of care moving on to other employment. Core church narratives were compared with those at Swindon, Govan, and Digswell to check for similarities and differences. In essence these narratives were used as additional factors to tease out or confirm themes. At Swindon, volunteers did not speak easily about their faith, compared to the intentional sharing of faith at Digswell. Findings regarding whether volunteers spoke of their faith from Swindon and Digswell were compared with data and emergent themes from Govan and Hope International/Northern Training. A link between core church narratives and volunteers talking about faith emerged during the study at Govan, leading to a reexamination of data from Swindon and Digswell that revealed a similar correspondence.

Ethnographic Methods

I needed to gain as full a picture as possible regarding both the immediate and wider contexts of each initiative. At Digswell I attended numerous church services, prayer meetings, meals, and other church events. This included visits to a homework club run by some of the volunteers, and a visit to their annual camp, which provided a holiday for the migrant women and their families. Immersion in the field setting was of primary importance and ethnographic methods served me well in understanding the connections and disconnections in each situation between what people believed and what they practiced, otherwise called lived and espoused theologies.[19] An ethnographic approach enabled full access to the phenomena studied and allowed for detailed observation and note-taking. Gaining a full

---

19. Moschella, "Ethnography," 224.

picture of the initiatives required me to spend a large amount of time with volunteers and in settings outside session times.

Ethnography is conducted in natural settings and involves live interactions with people and phenomena—in this case, the volunteers at the four initiatives. Ethnographers want to understand the world from the perspectives of those observed, as opposed to a specific theory or the researcher's own perspectives.[20] I understood the phenomena using triangulating methods that validated findings,[21] and ethnographic methods allowed long-term observation *in situ*. Context was added through interviews, document searches, and attendance at other church events.

Ethnography has its roots in symbolic interactionism. This posits that human interactions take place in a context that is given meaning by the people involved. This underlies my approach to GT and associated themes of meaning, action and interaction, self, and perspectives. It involves direct, continued experience with the people studied as a "participant observer."

After observing and recording numerous initiative sessions, I asked open questions when interviewing volunteers. These questions were based on my observations and preliminary, but tentative, analysis. For instance, one volunteer at Swindon appeared to have limited teaching ability and was apparently unprepared for lessons, so I asked what motivated him. His response both validated my initial hunches and provided further insights on motivation. Until data saturation was reached, detailed observations over an extended time also enabled me to understand how this participant contributed and in turn led to my valuing his contribution to the tutoring team. While not interested in teaching English, his contribution in setting up and clearing away after sessions was invaluable. Such methods give participants a voice and act as a corrective to researcher insight.

In addition to observing and interviewing, I hoped I would gain further insights from searches of church documents. These offered rich insights into volunteer motivations and behaviors at Swindon and Govan. Volunteer motivations and behaviors aligned with messages from pastors regarding the need to welcome outsiders and the importance of individually nurtured faith. These had been communicated often through bulletins and at church meetings. Data collected through observations and interviews should, where possible, be verified through documents and other sources.[22]

20. Schensul et al., *Initiating Ethnographic Research*, ch. 1.
21. Schwandt, *SAGE Dictionary of Qualitative Inquiry*, 297–98.
22. Schensul et al., *Initiating Ethnographic Research*, 26.

For contextual purposes many church documents were consulted in the first setting to complement observations and interviews with volunteers. This proved more difficult in other locations, although some documents were eventually provided. Consulting documents in tandem with interviewing church leaders enabled a broader understanding of context and provided thick data—a concept first described by Geertz.[23] Thick data reveals "'volunteers' views, feelings, intentions and actions . . . [through] writing extensive field notes of observations, collecting respondents' written personal accounts, finding relevant documents, and/or compiling detailed narratives (such as from transcribed tapes of interviews)."[24] The initiatives could only be interpreted from a theological perspective when they were considered within the context of local church life and teachings. Document searches through church records, therefore, identified core narratives that prompted participant conduct.

Thick data emerged from prolonged field observations, informal conversations with participants, semi-structured interviewing of participants and church leaders (with some questions based on observations specific to the interviewee), attendance at church services and other church events, and document searches. Data collected from as many angles as possible provided insights, such as a realization that core church narratives were at times reflected in the aims of the initiatives and participant behaviors. Obtaining thick data was an important process at Govan, where, although friendly, volunteers worked independently and without group prayer or planning. Sermons at church services I attended were about personal Christian growth, as were all the past bulletins I read. Conversations with Gideon, the pastor, indicated his concern to see individuals converted. While these concerns for individuals were all healthy, it seemed the result of this focus in church life was the formation of volunteers who did not appreciate the importance of working and growing as a team.

Methods of Data Collection

Data was gathered intentionally and methodically. For instance, I was careful to initially spend equal amounts of time observing each participant, while I would take more time to collect evidence to support or refute my hunches as needed. New theory was generated in this GT study through

23. Geertz, *Interpretation of Cultures*.
24. Charmaz, *Constructing Grounded Theory*, 23.

field notes from participant observation, interviews, and information from records and reports. GT emerged from careful study of real-life situations, using an iterative research process.

Interviews only commenced after observations had been conducted at numerous sessions. The delay allowed volunteers to become accustomed to a researcher being present and for me to develop rapport. This also afforded time to formulate questions around topics emerging from observations. During interviews, participants were encouraged to talk openly about the English classes, sewing club, and training school, and some questions were left deliberately vague to enable interviewees to talk about subjects that most interested them. Pastors were interviewed in each setting as a method for gaining rich background data. All interviewees were invited to discuss anything of importance as well as respond to direct, specific questions.

Theoretical sampling was conducted as themes, such as the interweaving of social action and evangelism at Swindon Baptist, emerged from the interview data. Theoretical sampling takes place when a researcher focuses on a process that they consider seemingly important. They then consider whether this is true in other settings that allow for comparisons of their perceptions.[25] For instance, subsequent interviewees were specifically asked whether they viewed the initiative being studied as an evangelistic activity. None, in this setting, believed it was or should be.

The Researcher within the Study

I have been formed by life events, relationships (positive and negative), and years of study. While I have processed some of this, I am, no doubt, unaware of assumptions and biases that have crept in over the years, based on these experiences. It is not possible for a researcher to be a neutral observer, try as we may. Self-understanding is, therefore, important and must play an appropriate role in the research process. The epistemological foundations for this study have been strongly influenced by critical reflections on my own journey of intercultural relating, as outlined already. The result was a post-foundationalist, critical-realist approach to analysis which rejects the absolute certainties of modernism and foundationalism.[26] Developing this

---

25. Engel and Schutt, *Practice of Research*, 282. The authors refer to Ragin, *Comparative Method*.

26. Macallan, *Postfoundationalist Reflections*, 25.

further, four aspects of post-foundationalism inform the epistemology that guided the data analysis.[27]

First, we form and strengthen beliefs from our interpretation of experiences. This feeds into networks of beliefs that in turn are applied to interpret further experiences. My autobiographical narrative to this book outlines the cross-cultural experiences that have shaped my thinking. Biases borne from experience resulted in my view that migrants from other religions were not necessarily "unsaved." This alerted me to what I now view as clumsy attempts at evangelism and to my own negative judgments of them.

Second, "the objective unity of truth is a necessary condition for the intelligible search for knowledge, and the subjective multiplicity of knowledge indicates the fallibility of truth claims."[28] Some volunteers seemed concerned that migrants from different religions will not experience salvation. Salvation may be understood differently among volunteers, who may take it to refer to either eternal destiny or salvation from challenging situations in this life. It may also mean that people of other religions might be eternally saved.

While the volunteers running the program may believe their approach is both theologically and culturally rational, attendees from other cultures may have a very different point of view. This illustrates that rational judgment is exercised within social contexts. A rich point of exploration that was anticipated was whether those running the initiative could respect others and appreciate their judgments as rational (whether these were understood or not), as well as appreciate that some of what they do may be considered irrational by those attending the initiatives.

Third, "explanation aims for universal, transcontextual understanding, and understanding derives from particular, contextualized explanations."[29] Even though the study involved only a small number of local cases, it was reasonable to expect that generalizable insights could be gained.

I was initially a guest at the four locations; while I had been given permission by the participants to attend the initiatives, I was otherwise unknown, and my presence was possibly threatening to some. Indeed, one volunteer at Swindon had declined to participate in the study, not wanting to be watched and risk—to her mind, perhaps—being judged unfavorably

---

27. Schults, *Postfoundationalist Task*, 43.
28. Schults, *Postfoundationalist Task*, 43.
29. Schults, *Postfoundationalist Task*, 43.

by me. I was surprised, however, by how quickly I was accepted as one of the group. A touching example of this was when the volunteers at Swindon gave me a card to mark a milestone birthday I celebrated during my time there.

When a researcher first arrives at a study location, they are a newcomer in that situation. They will not know what is considered correct behavior, and their presence may, therefore, be disruptive.[30] Initially, I was aware of the risk that people might change conversations and behaviors due to my presence. Prolonged time in the field setting, as detailed above, helped volunteers become accustomed to me being there. This settling, I believe, resulted in normal behaviors being observed. I aimed to mediate my presence in each setting by listening rather than speaking, by communicating respect for participant actions and opinions, by acknowledging and noting my responses and initial assessments while present, and by being prepared to evaluate my actions later.

The behavior of a field researcher is important for obtaining reliable data. Every attempt was made, therefore, to keep my role low profile. While I did speak with both volunteers and clients during sessions, I kept this to a minimum. I matched my style of dress to volunteers to avoid standing out, and I refrained from being as verbal as I would normally be. By helping in small ways and being as personable as possible, I sought to blend into the group. Many times, my Christian faith facilitated instant acceptance, although not all participants realized I was a practicing Christian. Viewing me as a fellow Christian led to some participants speaking freely about their own faith journeys. For example, at Swindon, once Jean had established during her interview that I was a practicing Christian, she found she wanted to say much more than she had initially, relating her faith journey to volunteering at the English classes.

Finally, no ethnographer is a blank slate. We all enter field settings with our own ideas, beliefs, and biases, which we are unable to completely bracket out. Ethnography is, therefore, both inductive and deductive because such prior knowledge or assumptions can assist in formulating an initial model about the study, which will make ethnographer bias explicit.[31] Of course, rigorous analytic processes can interpret and discriminate this fusion.

---

30. Schensul et al., *Initiating Ethnographic Research*, ch. 1.
31. Schensul et al., *Initiating Ethnographic Research*, 14–20.

PART 1

Sensitivity to our thoughts and biases may be gained by the practice of "presence."[32] The practice of reflective presence becomes an analytical discipline, enhancing researcher sensitivity. Past academic study, ministry as theologically reflective practice, and intercultural experiences have also helped me form researcher sensitivity. Biases can also be checked by the objective reality of data, supervision, and checking for accuracy with participants. Accordingly, care was taken in fieldwork settings to remain aware of my personal biases and to attempt to look beyond these by using the research disciplines of field notes, journaling, and supervision. Many personal reflexive comments were written during initial analysis.[33] These ranged from noting my surprise at something said or done, before thinking more deeply about the incident and looking for other possible interpretations. This process enabled me to be mindful of my responses to events. Attempts to overcome bias were made by seeking to identify participant behavior and attitudes contrary to norms previously identified.

Case Studies

This was initially a study of two, church-based, intercultural initiatives. The studies at Swindon and Digswell produced quite different data, and studies of further initiatives were, therefore, indicated. Studies of four locations enabled meaningful comparisons. For instance, I learned how participants were shaped by their respective core church narratives: each participant displayed their previous spiritual formation through their work or volunteering. By comparing four different situations, I conducted a multiple-case study. Exploratory case studies help answer the questions of how and why phenomena occur.

Study locations were chosen according to the following factors:

a. A church that regularly and historically planned and implemented a community initiative that attracted people from non-Australian cultures.

b. A volunteer staff largely made up of church members.

c. Volunteers previously unknown to the researcher.

d. Permission of the pastor/leaders to conduct research.

32. As defined in chapter 1.
33. Lempert, "Asking Questions of the Data."

e. Different denominations and different sociocultural areas of Melbourne.
f. A minimum of six volunteers for each location. It was hoped this would be an adequate number of volunteers to gain useful data. Only four completed the study at Digswell. It was decided to continue with this smaller cohort as useful data was still being generated. However, this situation indicated the need for further study locations.
g. A willingness of volunteers to participate in one-on-one interviews.
h. Appropriate permission to access church documents. Although permission was initially granted, full records were not always made available.

All congregations were self-described as evangelical, believing that salvation is only through Jesus Christ. Many evangelicals may assume, therefore, that the gospel message needs to be proclaimed in any way possible. This belief, in turn, may motivate study participants to use the initiative as a vehicle for evangelism. This idea was explored through the data, thus acting as a limited comparative study of the intended functions of church-based initiatives.

Interviews

Observations alone were unlikely to provide sufficient information for me to understand the dynamics at initiatives. I, therefore, needed to interview each participant to understand their beliefs and motivations. Interviews only commenced after observations had been conducted for numerous sessions. The delay allowed participants to become accustomed to a researcher being present and for me to develop rapport. This also afforded time to formulate questions around topics emerging from observations. I found that observation-driven, open questions were more culturally and contextually aware. Pastors were interviewed in each setting and the founder of the teaching program at Swindon Baptist was also interviewed. These interviews provided rich background data, especially when leaders spoke of how they saw the initiatives fit with the rest of church life and their aims for or assumptions about how they were conducted. At Swindon and Govan,

PART 1

pastors expressed their desires for initiatives to be a gateway into the broader life of the church, an aim not shared by many volunteers.

Interviews addressed the question "How is love of God and neighbor communicated effectively in the context of intercultural, church-based initiatives in four evangelical Melbourne churches?" The focus was upon motivations for volunteering, levels of intercultural awareness, understandings of evangelism, spirituality, and each participant's willingness and ability to learn and grow. Open-ended questions were tailored to each context and each interviewee, and specific questions were followed with further questions for clarification or depth. Many other areas were presented for consideration both through observations and interviews, as outlined in chapter 3 and discussed in chapters 5 through 7.

Observations at Church Services and Other Gatherings

As the initiatives were all extensions of church life, it was important for me to understand the wider church context. This would, I hoped, provide insight into beliefs and behaviors observed at initiatives. Ethnographers observe complex interactions, often interrelated, which they seek to unravel. Attending services provided background data, such as core church narratives, the opportunity to observe participants in a different context, and valuable data that shaped a thick description of the context in which services operated.[34]

All but three of the Swindon volunteers attended one of two English-language Sunday services. By attending one of these services at each Sunday visit, I observed volunteers before and after services to learn whether they interacted cross-culturally at these times. At Digswell, services were attended by up to thirty Syrian migrants, a small handful of estate residents (older singles, none of African descent), and up to ten members of other Digswell Anglican congregations. None of the women who attended the sewing club attended the meal or the church services. Attending the services allowed observation of volunteers interacting both formally and informally with people from language and culture groups beyond those who attended the sewing club. I attended four Bible studies led by two volunteers for some migrants at Govan Church of Christ, and this offered valuable insights into these volunteers. Four church services were attended at Hope International

---

34. Geertz, *Interpretation of Cultures*, 3–33.

Church and one graduation service, in addition to observations at English lessons.

CONCLUSION

This chapter has demonstrated my careful engagement with qualitative methods that include ethnographic methods and case study design to produce reliable data from the four initiatives. Detailed data was collected through observations, semi-structured interviews, and document searches. The flexibility of GT enabled me to follow where the data led, resulting in a shift from a solely missiological focus to one incorporating the disciplines of pastoral care, intercultural pastoral care, and missiology. Care was taken in field settings to conduct myself in a manner sensitive to the conduct of the research. This enabled me to have as little influence as possible on proceedings and interview answers, while noting that complete neutrality is difficult. Data analysis, conducted as the project unfolded, allowed me to follow up on new insights at two more locations. This allowed for the creation of robust theory.

QUESTIONS FOR REFLECTION AND DISCUSSION

- In what ways might we learn how well we are communicating love of God and neighbor at any church-based, intercultural initiatives we conduct?
- How can we be sure our observations are accurate? What else might we do to confirm this?

3

Models to Aid Intercultural Care

LOVE IS . . . A PRACTICAL DEMONSTRATION OF THE CHARACTER OF GOD

The following biblical reflections highlight the linking theme behind the focus of the research question—the love of God. They are neither exegesis nor commentary, homily nor exhortation, yet they introduce biblical and theological themes that each church in the study embraced and thus they allowed deeper interpretation of data. They are pastoral and theological reflections that enabled and informed integration of findings. They are inevitably selective given the enormous range of resources on this topic but were chosen to provide a working foundation. They were written after fieldwork was concluded, based on theological reflection, and written with the aim of demonstrating the biblical basis for the following discussions.

Luke 10:25–37: The Good Samaritan

This parable is the first of three passages that suggest interrelationships between caring for a neighbor and being intimately engaged with God. Our ethics emerge from our relationship with God. This pericope corresponds to passages in Mark 12:28–34 and Matt 22:34–40 where Jesus responds to the question about the greatest commandment. Jesus views this parable as an alternative response that demonstrates that love of neighbor "has the same force" and meaning as love for God.[1]

The parable addresses loving our neighbor even when in conflict and in a context of complex cultural and religious difference. Jesus illustrates how deeds, not just words or a set of beliefs, are foundational and inextricably linked to our call as children of God and to our capacity to go beyond the limits of difference or division. Our relationship with God can bring life in all contexts, something that neither works nor belief systems will achieve on their own. This parable aligns with the theme in Luke that the poor, which includes outcasts and foreigners, may all experience God's mercy.[2] The Samaritan traveler pauses to see how he could help the naked and clearly robbed man (v. 33). The Samaritan first chooses to approach the victim rather than walk on by. What he saw provoked compassion and a caring response.[3] This perhaps indicates the Samaritan's natural tendency to care for all, not just those from his own people group. Taking the time to see if others need assistance and determining what this assistance should be are first steps towards loving others.

Having ascertained that the man needed assistance, the Samaritan tenderly cares for him. Jesus notes that this was done out of compassion (v. 33), a simple model of compassionate care. The Samaritan goes the second mile by taking the man to an inn, where he delegates his care for him, just as now, when we quite normally delegate care to others or agencies. This hopefully avoids the commodification of need or the medicalizing of care. Care must set limits, and referral to others is often appropriate and necessary. Likewise, the Samaritan left the injured man in the care of another. This story demonstrates an unlikely coming together of people, uncommon trust of one another, and service. This trust includes the deal between the Samaritan and the innkeeper. These unusual partnerships carry risk by which the victim of crime benefits. This illustrates the reign of God.[4] Such momentary glimpses emerged at each intercultural initiative where, in Samaritan mode, everyone is welcome and where the organizing of resources has both corporate and community characteristics.

---

1. Johnson, *Gospel of Luke*, 174–75.
2. Evans, *Luke*, 177.
3. Johnson, *Gospel of Luke*, 173.
4. Longenecker, "Story of the Samaritan."

PART 1

John 4:4–42: The Woman at the Well

Jesus' mission was not limited to the Jews.[5] Considering the tensions between the Samaritans and the Jews, walking through Samaria may have required courage.[6] These actions demonstrate the heart of God.[7] Jesus and his disciples were a minority group that had moved into the margins of society, arguably the current perception and role of the church in many Western countries.[8] His willingness to talk to a despised Samaritan, a woman, broke religious and social protocol, especially as he, and no doubt others, knew her history and current living arrangements.[9] In this action, Jesus practiced ministry from the margins to the margins and demonstrated the hospitable heart of God by suggesting to the woman that she would have turned to God had she known God's character (v. 10). Jesus may have been aware that this radical encounter could potentially change the whole community, then and now, in its attitudes to those completely other (John 4:28–30, 39–42). Within a frame of mutual hospitality that aligns with practice at the initiatives, refugees and asylum seekers are one context where the ministry of Christians prospers or fails through its hospitality.[10]

When the woman asks to know God's love, Jesus offers a relationship that is without pretense or cheap grace and invites her to confront her lifestyle. Significant by omission, Jesus did not tell the woman to leave her partner. This is not the point of the story; rather, we are not to erect barriers or set priorities that block others from relationship with God. She knew that he knew her marital status, but this was not the priority of the moment. This is an example of the woman's dependence on or manipulation of men for survival.[11] Changing our lifestyles is a result, not a prerequisite, of encountering God. This story foreshadows the later ministry of the disciples, as well as the calling of modern-day disciples.[12]

---

5. Thompson, *John*, 98.
6. Thompson, *John*, 99.
7. Grayston, *Gospel of John*, 40.
8. See Frost, *Exiles*, 6.
9. Malina and Rohrbaugh, *Social-Science Commentary on John*, 105.
10. Langmead, "Refugees as Guests and Hosts," 29.
11. Grayston, *Gospel of John*, 42.
12. Thompson, *John*, 106.

John 13:1–17: Jesus Washes the Disciples' Feet

Jesus washed the feet of his disciples, normally the work of a slave, in a symbolic display of God's intention to serve.[13] Willingness to perform the humble, menial, and unpleasant task of foot-washing modeled servanthood for his disciples,[14] and reflected how Christians should not prioritize themselves over others (Phil 2:3). By washing the disciples' feet, Jesus indicates the radical difference in his values to those of the society around him.[15] This action challenges volunteers to reflect upon whether they consider themselves in any way superior to new or temporary migrants attending the initiatives and addresses the power they have as hosts and as holders of knowledge and resources.

John 13:13 states that Jesus loved his disciples to the end. His commitment was absolute. He did not stay with them just because they were useful. At a time when his anxiety would have been mounting in the face of his impending death, he chose instead to focus on the disciples, even when confronted with possible betrayal. This demonstration of God's love is certainly far beyond the scope of the initiatives, yet nevertheless indicates the need for a high level of commitment to relationship.

These pericopes introduce major themes of care, two of which are in intercultural settings. The parable of the good Samaritan and the pericope about Jesus and the woman at the well both speak of risk. Volunteers took risks in crossing cultural and linguistic boundaries to offer care to strangers. Risk is, to some extent, mitigated through education and reflective practice. This theme of nurtured, reflective care resonated with my findings and suggested a framework for analysis based in intercultural pastoral care.

An interrelated theme to emerge at each initiative was the intercultural aspects of care, echoed in the story of the good Samaritan and in Jesus' interaction with the woman at the well. By crossing cultural boundaries and engaging with the woman, Jesus potentially changed a community. He risked his own reputation to express care and did not place demands on the woman that were out of reach in her context. Successfully crossing cultural boundaries will benefit from guidance, and models of intercultural competence offer this.

---

13. Thompson, *John*, 282.
14. Thompson, *John*, 282.
15. Malina and Rohrbaugh, *Social-Science Commentary on John*, 221.

Having collected field notes, interviews, information from documents, and having spent time at services and other church-based events, I formed a picture of the way in which volunteers express love, their motivations for service, and their skills at the four locations. I formed tentative hypotheses, abandoned some, and strengthened others. It became clear that volunteers were offering intercultural pastoral care to the people attending initiatives and that mission and evangelism were either not prioritized, or in the case of Digswell, conflicted with the volunteers' abilities to offer care. Frameworks for the provision of intercultural pastoral care and intercultural competence were important considerations for understanding the data and for suggesting improved practice. These themes are echoed in these biblical passages.

LARTEY'S FRAMEWORK FOR INTERCULTURAL PASTORAL CARE

The third pericope above recounts Jesus' care for his disciples by describing Jesus taking the role of a servant when he washed the disciples' feet. Volunteers also became servant-carers when they taught English, sewing, childcare, and cared in numerous other ways that presented in these relational contexts.

Given the research question, an organizing principle behind data analysis self-evidently required a theological and pastoral framework. Lartey's model of intercultural pastoral care complemented the emerging data by providing a clearer focus on the essential elements: expressions of human concern through activities, recognition of transcendence, and acknowledgment of varying forms of communication—all essentially motivated by love and aiming to prevent harm and foster wellbeing.[16] Participants were attempting to navigate the similarities and differences between themselves and the migrants attending initiatives. Lartey associates a number of terms with the dynamics of intercultural pastoral care theory and practice: globalization, internationalization, and indigenization.[17] He suggests that the discipline(s) of pastoral care is (are) becoming tailored to the global situations of practice, recognizing that Western paradigms are not necessarily applicable or effective in different cultural contexts.

---

16. Lartey, *In Living Color*, 5–9.
17. Lartey, "Globalization, Internationalization, and Indigenization."

Data analysis indicated that a desire to demonstrate pastoral care, as defined above, was a strong motivator among volunteers in the fieldwork settings. Lartey's framework for pastoral care, developed in a cross-cultural context and placed in dialogue with Augsburger's definition of a culturally competent counselor,[18] was, therefore, considered the most suitable analytical framework. Lartey was brought into analytical consideration following fieldwork and a provisional sorting of findings at the first location. His understandings were not applied (as far as possible) to the sorting of data of subsequent findings. Sorting and categorizing findings (done by means of coding) was an intense process at each location, and I focused on patterns emerging through coding rather than theoretical explanations.

Chapters 6 to 9 will explore Lartey's framework further in relation to findings at the four initiatives. Care can be understood as ministry, social action, empowerment, and as personal interaction—all themes at the initiatives.[19] The functions of pastoral care, briefly introduced in chapter 1, will be examined in relation to the initiatives in chapter 6. Lartey applies characteristics of counseling to pastoral care practices, emphasizing the importance of carers fostering a sense of self-in-relationship.[20] The pedagogical cycle for liberative practice, based in liberation theologies, has applications for intercultural care. It encourages carers to reflect theologically, with experience as the starting point, rather than imposing biblical understandings onto situations in which care is practiced.[21] These aspects of the framework will be explored in chapter 9. Lartey's emphasis on spirituality for pastoral care offers rich points of learning for initiative participants. He explores five dimensions of spirituality, most of which have application for the delivery of effective care at the initiatives. These are discussed in chapter 7.

INTERCULTURAL COMPETENCE

Almost all volunteers were attempting to communicate care across cultural divides. Models of intercultural competence help us understand the dimensions of culture to which we must adjust our understanding and behaviors if we are to do this successfully. This section introduces models of intercultural competence that were engaged in analysis. Intercultural communication

18. Augsburger, *Pastoral Counseling*, 20–22.
19. Lartey, *In Living Color*, 59.
20. Lartey, *In Living Color*, 81–111.
21. Lartey, *In Living Color*, 113–39.

adds layers of complexity to human interactions. If we are to communicate love of God and neighbor, we must move beyond considerations of what we say and do to how our words and actions might be received by others. What may seem to be a clear communication on the part of one person is open to misinterpretation by someone from another culture. Dave, the pastor at Digswell, understood that it was not culturally appropriate for him to chat with the women who attended the sewing club. This knowledge was coupled with his willingness not to offend. Rather than assert his culturally informed belief that men and women should be free to interact, he indicated a high level of intercultural competence by refraining from interaction. Respect for the beliefs of others communicated his love of God and neighbor.

Intercultural competence supports the practice of intercultural pastoral care and mission. Jesus understood enough about the cultural differences between Jews and Samaritans to speak meaningfully to the woman at the well. The Samaritan stopped, observed, and thoughtfully offered care to the man at the roadside. Models of cultural competence teach us to do this too. Livermore argues that Cultural Intelligence (CQ), a form of cultural competence, enables us to love the other.[22] Although literature regarding intercultural competence may not have been directly or consistently applied to pastoral care and mission, different models of intercultural competence all supported successful intercultural communication. The term "intercultural competence" will be used generically in the discussion that follows, with particular attention to the CQ model, a model added to the methods of data analysis. This model has been discussed in relation to mission,[23] and certainly intercultural competence has a natural affinity with intercultural initiatives, both for mission and pastoral care. This brief discussion of different models of intercultural competence suggests a context for a survey of the CQ model.

Ting-Toomey proposes that appropriateness, effectiveness, and communication can be used to measure transcultural communicative competence and the inherent components of knowledge, mindfulness, and communication skills.[24] This resonates with the basic "checking modes" of reflective practice, theological reflection, and praxis—all important disciplines for Christians engaged in intercultural settings. For example, the Standards of Practice document of Spiritual Care Australia requires at least ten hours of supervision for health care chaplains. It also requires chaplains

22. Livermore, *Cultural Intelligence*, 45–56.
23. Livermore, *Cultural Intelligence*.
24. Ting-Toomey, *Communicating across Cultures*.

to respect and cooperate with the provision of care for clients from diverse religious and cultural backgrounds.[25] Spitzberg suggests a model of intercultural competence that he claims is consistent with the extant theoretical and empirical literature. This integrative model sees knowledge and skills interact, as individual motivation and self-perception are revealed in a context where a person influences interaction with a second person.[26] Self-awareness and mindfulness may add clearer definition to this model by acknowledging the importance of motivation inspired by God's love, self-perception supported by intrapersonal spirituality, and the ability to reflect theologically on practice. These essential skills and practices complement, for ministry and formation purposes, the sensitivities developed within CQ.

Models of Intercultural Competence

Cultural Intelligence

Cultural Intelligence (CQ) has found traction within mission circles in recent years. Tang, Earley, and Ang developed their theory of Cultural Intelligence[27] based on the "Four loci of intelligence" theory of Sternberg and Detterman.[28] The theory borrows from research in IQ and has four domains: cognitive, metacognitive, motivational, and behavioral. Cognitive CQ concerns a person's cross-cultural knowledge, while metacognitive CQ describes a person's ability to think and apply this knowledge during a cross-cultural interaction. Motivational CQ refers to an individual's emotional capacity and energy to learn about how to conduct themselves in cross-cultural settings, and behavioral CQ is about the ability to adapt speech and nonverbal behaviors in cross-cultural settings.[29] Each domain has sub-domains, and CQ exists to the extent that each of these domains are operative.

Intelligence theorists have influenced each theoretical category of the CQ framework. Ackerman argued that knowledge should be considered a part of a person's intellect.[30] Motivational CQ was developed out of the

---

25. See Spiritual Care Australia, "Standards of Practice," 13.
26. Spitzberg, "Model of Intercultural Communication."
27. Earley et al., CQ. This early model had three domains, soon extended to four. See Ang and Van Dyne, "Conceptualizations of Cultural Intelligence," 3–16.
28. Sternberg and Detterman, *What Is Intelligence?*
29. Ang and Van Dyne, "Conceptualizations of Cultural Intelligence," 5–6.
30 Ackerman, "Adult Intellectual Development."

work of Ceci, who published his theory of Real World Intelligence.[31] This theory posits that problem-solving capacities need to be activated and that an individual requires the motivation for this. Behavioral intelligence is the basis for the concept of behavioral CQ and refers to the capacity of an individual to display culturally acceptable outward behaviors. Hall describes this as a necessary complement to cognitive and motivational capabilities.[32]

Livermore's consideration of the CQ framework for mission is significant for this study as it concerns how we can effectively communicate with people from different cultures. In *Cultural Intelligence* he both starts and concludes his discussion of the CQ framework with a discussion of "love of the other" as the motivation for Christians to develop CQ.[33] He bases this argument on a brief consideration of the incarnation, suggesting that the CQ framework does not require love for efficacy. Where love is a starting point for intercultural interactions, the other considerations for pastoral care and mission surveyed in this chapter will play a more central role, a criterion applied to evaluating the effectiveness of each initiative. For example, the biblical basis for both disciplines is a point of inspiration and motivation. Considerations regarding the incarnation, as suggested by Livermore, are based on the biblical accounts of Jesus' examples of love-in-action. Other biblical accounts model approaches to pastoral care and mission, including those explored by Peterson and noted above.[34]

Other Models of Intercultural Competence

Models of intercultural competence originate in the disciplines of psychology, communication, and education. Martin suggests three important factors for future research into cultural competency that were integral to the projects studied in this book: develop a more holistic, spiritual, and relational view of intercultural competence, acknowledge the fluid dimensions of culture, and interact with the fact that all cross-cultural interactions contain a power dimension.[35] These are all key themes for effective pastoral care.

Theories of intercultural competence lack one of the elements most vital for mission because they are not rooted in love. Livermore adds to the CQ

---

31. Ceci, *On Intelligence*.
32. Hall, *Silent Language*.
33. Livermore, *Cultural Intelligence*, 33–35.
34. Peterson, *Five Smooth Stones*.
35. Martin, "Revisiting Intercultural Competence."

model by including love,[36] but it does not appear relevant for other authors. Without at least genuine interest in others, models of intercultural competence may be challenged as conflicted by undeclared goals and self-interest.

Moreau, Hay Campbell, and Greener outline ways of developing intercultural competence by briefly reviewing four models of intercultural competency specifically designed to aid the practice of cross-cultural mission: cognitive awareness model, character traits model, social skills model, and interactionist model.[37] Although the work of Livermore and the CQ model is mentioned,[38] the authors do not dwell on this, referring to it as one model among others.[39] Notably, again via the CQ channel, these models align with formational themes of self-awareness, spiritual nurture, and the acquisition of interpersonal skills, particularly the cross-cultural pastoral counseling sector.

Augsburger, like Lartey, develops his discussion of intercultural considerations for pastoral carers and counselors around Kluckhohn and Murray's theory of humanness.[40] He believes that all peoples are more alike than they are different, outlining four global constants in humans: biological similarity, psychological commonality, spiritual similarities, and parallel patterning in sociocultural structures.[41] Regarding the fact that we are all similar in many ways, he notes that

> the relationship between sociocultural variables and psychological variables is one of the most intriguing and important questions in intercultural research.... Anthropologists have been primarily concerned with the impact of culture on personality, psychologists with the variables of psychic formation and functioning.[42]

Augsburger names six relationships between these variables: culture is personality, personality is culture, personality creates culture, personality mediates culture, personality and culture are parallel systems, and personality and culture are parts of an organic system.[43] Regarding "like no other

---

36. Livermore, *Cultural Intelligence*, 17–20.
37. Moreau et al., *Effective Intercultural Communication*.
38. Livermore, *Cultural Intelligence*.
39. Moreau et al., *Effective Intercultural Communication*.
40. Kluckhohn and Murray, "Personality in Nature," 35, referred to in Augsburger, *Pastoral Counseling*, 49.
41. Augsburger, *Pastoral Counseling*, 55–56.
42. Augsburger, *Pastoral Counseling*, 61.
43. Augsburger, *Pastoral Counseling*, 62.

[person]," he notes that "every human being is unique, a unique world of perceptions, feelings, and experience. No other person will ever see, think, feel, celebrate, or suffer in [an] identical way."[44] These relationships nuance models of cultural competence, reflecting the principles of person-centered care within a pastoral care mode. They inform data analysis and interpretation by reminding us that individual personalities exist beyond cultural norms and by reminding us to celebrate others as unique individuals. They also provide an additional rationale for training and formation in the skills and knowledge that undergird pastoral and mission practice.

Lartey adds a valuable note, suggesting that intercultural pastoral care should complement Kluckhohn and Murray's domains: "In order to gain a fuller understanding of human persons within the global community, it is necessary to explore the ways in which culture, individual uniqueness, and human characteristics work together to influence persons."[45] He warns against using research into different cultures to reduce persons to a set of behaviors rather than considering them as unique individuals.[46] The approaches taken by Augsburger and Lartey to intercultural exchanges in pastoral care contain the potential for significantly more in-depth relating than the CQ model.

Gittins describes a postmodern understanding of culture:

> Definitions now tend to romanticize culture much less [than traditionally], to minimize the scientific nature of anthropology itself in favour of a more "interpretative" approach to cultural manifestations, and to view cultures not as discrete or static entities but as constantly "contested" (a helpful notion, this) by their members, who struggle to reinvent themselves, to make new choices, or simply to survive.[47]

When a researcher first arrives at a study location, they will not know what is considered correct behavior and their presence may, therefore, be disruptive.[48] Gittins, Lartey, and Augsburger are concerned with the real-life individuals with whom we seek to build relationships.[49] This is an

---

44. Augsburger, *Pastoral Counseling*, 49.
45. Lartey, *In Living Color*, 171.
46. Lartey, *In Living Color*, 165–74.
47. Gittins, *Living Mission Interculturally*, 45.
48. Schensul et al., *Initiating Ethnographic Research*, ch. 1.
49. Gittins, *Living Mission Interculturally*; Lartey, *In Living Color*; Augsburger, *Pastoral Counseling*.

ethically robust approach to cultural competence, which enables love of God and neighbor to become an important factor in a manner lacking in the cultural competence models noted above.

Writing in the sphere of Catholic social action, Arbuckle addresses those working among different cultures, such as the participants in this study.[50] He offers guidelines for ministering within a mode of meaning-making evangelization which, as noted earlier, reveals a more holistic and systemic approach, contrasting with evangelism to people of different cultures—a more amenable word within the context of the various projects. The practice of inculturation for Christians working with migrants works best when informed of the stages of migrant adjustment to a new culture. This enables practitioners to discern what different pastoral action might be employed in light of migrant experiences.[51] This is a high-level pastoral and missions skill.

While there are many aspects in common, no consensus is necessary regarding any model of intercultural competence. A starting point for the acquisition of cultural competence is perhaps found in the "radical respect for alterity" described by Doehring as a key pastoral skill or stance.[52] The CQ model does not require this, although it would be a valuable component. Both mission and pastoral care require such respect to communicate love to migrants. These factors enabled data analysis to determine that neither respect for alterity nor cultural competence were clearly understood or knowingly expressed at the initiatives.

QUESTIONS FOR REFLECTION AND DISCUSSION

- Identify two Bible passages that demonstrate intercultural pastoral care. Discuss any insights gained that might be applied to church-based initiatives.
- In what ways do I need to grow in intercultural competence? What resources would help this process?

---

50. Arbuckle, *Earthing the Gospel*, 187–206.
51. Arbuckle, *Earthing the Gospel*, 61–73.
52. Doehring, *Practice of Pastoral Care*, 1–4.

4

Learning to Love

Anthea and her students at Govan sat together, laughing and enjoying one another's company. Despite being a timid person, Anthea came alive during sessions. I watched her gently place her hand on that of her female student, as she listened to her speak in halting English. Volunteering at English classes seemed a good fit for Anthea, an observation strengthened during her interview, when she spoke of the meaning that her relationships with those attending classes had brought her. These relationships were a joy to observe, and I reflected on how we can prosper when we act according to our gifts.

ON-THE-GROUND REALITIES

This chapter will outline what I discovered "on the ground" at each of the initiatives. My findings are representative of what may be found at other church-based initiatives and other missions projects. Three major themes emerged from my study of the four initiatives. These are: expressions of love, of motivations, and of skills. Participants demonstrated love in many ways, although at times love failed, for instance when a volunteer lost her temper with an attendee. Motivations for service were expressed during interviews and were also seen to drive certain behaviors during initiatives. Skills refers to both skills necessary for running the initiative and inter-relating skills.

This chapter lays the foundation for the following chapters, which explore what I found in greater depth and suggest ways in which learning might be applied at church-based, intercultural initiatives and in other mission situations.

SWINDON BAPTIST: ENGLISH CLASSES

All volunteer English tutors were in their fifties, sixties, or seventies. Deb, a migrant from Hong Kong, coordinated the sessions. Jason, her husband, didn't enjoy teaching his students but also helped set up and pack up. Jean was originally from India and had lived in several countries. Married couple Kay and Matt volunteered weekly, together with Chris, Jim, Karen, and Sandy. Unlike relationships at Northern Training, Swindon tutors only met together once during class terms, although several tutors regularly shared coffee after lessons. Some met briefly on a Sunday at English language services. During the observation period there was only a half-hour planning meeting opened briefly by prayer, the only time prayer was witnessed among the volunteers. None spoke of their Christian faith during interviews, unless directly asked. God was referenced indirectly by some when asked how their faith motivated them, but for the most part God had gone underground. Cordial conversation among tutors after class revealed no indications of mutual care among volunteers during or outside classes. Tutors were polite but reserved with students. This did not appear to hinder teaching, but it kept most relationships superficial.

Some volunteers only wanted to teach English, while others offered students any care they could. Teamwork and coordination appeared absent. At a formal, church level however, English language worship services had large attendances and were structured around band-led worship, preaching, visiting missionary testimony, or audiovisual presentations.

In summary, although friendly and welcoming, volunteers at Swindon seldom, if ever, talked about God and faith. Planning and group prayer were almost completely absent, and although friendly, little mutual care between volunteers was evident.

Personal theologies of mission were implied or stated by volunteers and came from explorations of participant motivation and observations of speech and actions. Karen described the purpose of the English classes as "a community service and as what I call pre-evangelism." She wanted to use the lessons to build relationships that might in time result in sharing the gospel.

PART 1

All but two volunteers connected volunteering with their Christian faith, although some connections only emerged from closer analysis. One spoke of her desire to simply be a blessing in whatever way she could. Another expressed a need to serve in some capacity in the church, while another described tutoring as a way of getting to know others in the church. Sandy hoped that "her faith [shone] through"; Chris hoped he "reflect[ed] God's love." Karen, a tutor who occasionally invited students to church social events, commented, "I'm someone who believes the gospel is not successful if it's rammed down other people's throats. I'm definitely of the opinion that you live your faith and opportunities arise that way and that is certainly what has happened." Other than these comments, volunteers did not speak directly of a desire to evangelize or aim for converts. They did speak of wanting to love others through what they were doing.

Despite classes having run for many years, the question of evangelism during classes had only recently been raised. Evangelism and conversion were not mentioned unless asked about during interviews. No one believed that evangelism should take place directly during classes, and one participant stated that teaching English should be the only activity. Two volunteers hoped for opportunities to invite students to church events, while Sandy stated that she hoped people experienced God's love through them. None used missional language (such as talking about conversions) when describing motivations for volunteering.

Significantly and unexpectedly, a motivation of pastoral care was considerably more evident than an evangelistic motivation among tutors. Volunteers did not speak about their own faith experiences with each other or students. While it would usually have been inappropriate in front of students, it was anticipated that volunteers would at least identify themselves as Christians on occasion. Chris said that, if asked, he would tell students he attends church, but when asked if this had ever happened, he replied that it had not. Relationship with God might have been the most important aspect of these volunteers' lives, but this was not verbally communicated even when several tutors socialized after classes. Even if volunteers wished to directly share the love of God with students, this was unlikely to be expressed in words. These attitudes stand in clear contrast to the senior pastor's expressed hope that the program would be a means by which attendees heard about God's love.

Group prayer was almost entirely absent. As noted, tutors met together just once, for a planning meeting, with Deb opening with a brief prayer. She used to have more meetings with tutors, but she had received several requests to curtail them. Tutors did not mention prayer at all during interviews. Group reflective practice was absent, as was both spiritual and practical supervision, whether formal or informal.

Although overt expressions of spirituality seem to have been privatized among this group, they were faithful in their service and care towards students. Three interviewees spoke indirectly of their faith as a motivation for volunteering. However, talking about God seemed to have been taboo, even though there were no ethical or professional constraints as in secular community support groups. I did not hear the name of Jesus mentioned once among this group. Accordingly, the spirituality of volunteers at Swindon could perhaps be described as quietly private. While inscrutable in religious terms, closer analysis revealed expressions of spirituality in behavior and motivation, and in identifiable pastoral themes.

Churches have defining or core narratives by which they are shaped, both official and unofficial. A comprehensive search of church minutes and bulletins revealed strong core narratives at Swindon. The senior pastor had held this post for thirty-seven years and regularly expressed his passion for congregational outreach ministries. "Welcoming others in the name of Jesus" was a phrase he had commonly used during meetings and often repeated in bulletin articles as he encouraged the congregation to works of service. He also emphasized during an interview his desire for the church to be multicultural and represent the local cultural demographic. His approach to multiculturalism came from his own background, the views of the former senior pastor, and the local demographics. The narrative of welcoming others in the name of Jesus emerged in English classes, reflecting the pastor's desire for a multicultural congregation serving the local community. Despite this, only two tutors were ever observed mixing with Asian or Nigerian church attendees after services. There was a continuing level of ambivalence among volunteers about mixing cross-culturally, unless the tutor was acting in a specific role, such as English tutor. The core narratives of welcoming others in the name of Jesus from a multicultural church base had filtered into day-to-day church activities to a large extent (numerous weekly English classes plus two East Asian and a Nigerian congregation), although deep levels of connection remained largely elusive.

Volunteers displayed cultural competence to varying degrees. Most volunteers declared a motivation for volunteering based on empathy towards migrants, because volunteers had lived overseas, had a family member from overseas, or had tried to learn a foreign language. Intercultural competence, including Cultural Intelligence (CQ), can be improved by educational and overseas trips, when an individual engages in the experiences.[1] These links were expressed overtly. There were also inconsistencies. One migrant displayed almost no interest in his students. Three volunteers who did not appeal to any of these experiences as a motivation also expressed less interest in the lives of their students. A much larger sample size would be necessary to draw any strong conclusions, but the theme emerged in other initiatives.

Knowledge of the cultural origins of students appeared to be limited, possibly indicating a lack of training and preparation for intercultural service. One participant said she did not need to know about student culture, as they were there to learn English. Only Jean understood that different learning and teaching styles exist among different cultures. However, about half the tutors checked that students understood their lessons and consequently adapted communication to suit learning needs. This displayed cultural competence through adaptive capacity. Other tutors appeared less self-aware when students appeared to switch off during lessons, unnoticed by the tutor. Higher-level thinking enabled tutors to understand a little of what students may be experiencing both during lessons and in their day-to-day lives, thereby more accurately assessing how they might meet their needs, an indication of instances of metacognitive CQ.

Various modes and levels of intercultural competence, therefore, appeared inconsistently, and no volunteers appeared to have theoretical or expressed knowledge of the competencies that would help them relate well to students. Relating across cultures was, therefore, expressed through trial and error and seemed to work through goodwill and kindness. The former cultural experiences of volunteers, plus an apparently generally high level of intelligence among tutors may have contributed to their competencies being as high as they were. Analysis of coding indicated that for most identified instances of high CQ, a contrasting instance of low CQ was noted.

Unfortunately, there was no reflective group dialogue or opportunity for learning from this discrepancy. Two tutors regularly taught in the manner of a distant expert, while another would regularly ask students for their opinion as equals. Some were better than others at carefully choosing words when addressing students. Intercultural competencies were not taught during the short training course before tutors were permitted to teach, and

1. Van Dyne et al., "Four Factor Model," 297.

no ongoing reflective practice offered opportunities to learn and improve. The brief course was clearly insufficient. There was no professional development or action/reflection that would have enabled volunteers to learn from each other and improve levels of cultural knowledge. Listening to the experiences of others may have fostered empathy. All volunteers indicated they were capable of metacognition, but this skill was not applied to teaching skills with appropriate training and reflection.

If, however, an underlying aim of possessing cultural competence was to better demonstrate love of God and neighbor, some tutors did succeed and effectively communicated love by listening, forming friendships with students, practicing hospitality, encouraging and praising students, proactively helping students, and (when appropriate) giving physical touch, such as hugs. It may be that these indications of love compensated for a lack of intercultural competencies in tutors, for students were observed responding warmly. Simple, basic pastoral care seemed to work, and "neighbor" could be a useful term to describe the relationships, though the idea of an informed and educated neighbor was not evident.

These volunteers displayed unmet potential. A high level of cross-cultural experience had created empathy for aspects of the migrant experience, although cultural knowledge regarding students remained low. Further education would have instilled this knowledge. High intercultural skills would have been born from training and reflection if coupled with the intelligence and experience of these volunteers. The ability of some volunteers to express love despite low cultural competence challenges the sufficiency of cultural competence models for Christian witness in that it seemed possible to communicate love effectively across cultures without having high cultural competence.

Summary of Significant Themes at Swindon

Empathy was clearly evident and is an expression of love. It was often noted both as a motivation for volunteering and in the compassionate way tutors spoke of their students. This was also observed during classes, as in Sandy's case, who would offer focused attention, smile, and engage with students with warmth. Again, most volunteers referred to occasions in their own lives when they had experienced the challenges of living overseas or of relating to migrants. Tutors also displayed great interest in getting to know their students personally, tending to see students as individuals, rather than

PART 1

objectifying them according to their culture of origin. This was indicative of love in that volunteers cared enough to want to know a particular student. Friendliness towards students reflects the church's core narrative of welcoming the local community into the church.

Given the complete absence of group reflection and prayer, the spirituality of volunteers was largely inscrutable or unseen, and the researcher often needed to look for clues behind statements or actions. The valuing of others expressed by Sandy through her actions, coupled with her statement that she "hopes her faith shines through" became an indicative benchmark. Volunteers may have seen their actions as loving towards others because of having experienced the love of Jesus. Some tutors implied this. Jim stated, "because I'm a Christian I'm bound to serve in some way, to recognize my faith in Christ. Then I need to take action." The lack of verbalization of faith, however, meant that this possible correlation was not explicit. Many demonstrations of the fruit of the Spirit, or loving attitudes expressed through pastoral care, were instead much clearer indicators of spirituality. Galatians 5:22–23 lists the fruit of the Spirit as "love, joy, peace, forbearance, kindness, goodness, faithfulness, gentleness, and self-control."

Volunteers often said they enjoyed meeting and being friends with people of other cultures because love was offered with no agenda attached. This may have been an outworking of faith or indicative of a lack of direct concern about evangelism, perhaps because volunteers felt it was inappropriate. The desire to be a multicultural church may well have influenced the establishment and running of the classes, but this was not verbalized by any volunteers, including the founder. Volunteers were unclear about the place of evangelism in class.

Motivations for service were varied. A desire to empower was frequently noted through interviews and observations, followed by personal satisfaction. However, the motivations of pastors (three of whom I interviewed) and volunteers at Swindon were different. Everyone wanted to empower migrants as they adapted to life in Australia by teaching English and helping in various ways, but the senior and youth pastors both hoped that evangelism would take place either during or because of classes, in contrast to most volunteers, who did not want this.

Both positive and poor communication skills were noted in roughly equal measure, perhaps reflecting a random selection of tutors not engaged in ongoing skill development. This indicates that the project leaders were not intentional about tutor training and skill development. Another contrasting finding was the presence of high and low levels of self-awareness. Self-awareness, or learning opportunities based on positive or negative experiences and feedback, was not nurtured among volunteers in their teaching and interpersonal skills. It may also be indicative of low engagement in spiritual formation within church life. While the importance of formation is explored in this book, there was insufficient evidence within this part of the data to support a conclusion, but enough to warrant additional research. However, since the team of volunteers only met together once for planning a half hour before a session started, and given the absence of shared prayer, enabling a culture and environment of reflection and formation is another factor worth considering.

Displays of empathy and care through words or actions were common. For example, in describing challenges for new migrants, Jean said (of her overseas experience), "Everything is different. Everything is strange. Not as strange as it would have been for [students], but nevertheless, there's an issue of coming into a new culture."

Sandy welcomed students warmly, but this was not representative of other volunteers who usually chatted apart from students before they were sorted into groups for classes. Volunteers were, however, friendly during lessons, and some students were spoken of with compassion by tutors, especially Karen, Chris, and Matt. They respected the fact that female students were highly educated and recognized the struggles in coming to Australia with their children.

Empathy for migrants and personal satisfaction were common motivations for volunteering. Motivations tended to be intrinsic, and enjoyment appeared to correlate with a desire to facilitate the good of others. Enjoying helping people from other language backgrounds and enjoying cross-cultural friendships are both marks of high motivational intelligence in the CQ model.[2] Some spoke of a sense of obligation to serve, as when Jean stated, "My faith compels me." Given her noted empathy for migrants, this statement implied understanding of the connection between belief and practice, rather than a sense of burden.

High and low levels of communication skills were present in roughly equal amounts, possibly indicating a lack of initial training and absence of supervision or ongoing development. Skill levels were probably high for some due to the strong levels of emotional intelligence and a high level of previous life experience. Higher-level thinking was apparent when previous

---

2. See Livermore, *Cultural Intelligence*.

learning was applied to current tasks. Administrative oversight failed to ensure regular group planning and prayer, and, in fact, administration was limited to sorting out which students were placed with which tutors.

DIGSWELL ANGLICAN CHURCH: SEWING CLUB

This was a smaller study than Swindon, while still providing helpful information. Joy had run the club for the past twelve years, assisted by Nancy, who was married to Dave, the pastor. Janet, a younger woman in her twenties, assisted as part of her church-based cross-cultural training. Community life among volunteers was more evident than at Swindon or Govan. Meaningful interactions each Sunday before the club strengthened a shared sense of mission. Prayer beforehand included all volunteers, and relationship dynamics were considered, as when one volunteer worked to counterbalance the negative input of another. Nancy would quietly come alongside the women to chat, and once, in front of the women, she gently teased Joy for being opinionated. Joy's desire to help the women was not always reflected in her manner, as when her style of address and frustrations eclipsed her generous heart. This harshness of expression was a major theme at the sewing club but not addressed through review or reflective practice. Significantly, there was no opportunity to do this.

Care among church members was apparent between sewing club volunteers, who were noted for expressing mutual affection. However, these friendships were exclusive, with conversations only occurring between volunteers, who talked over the heads of the women attending the club. This tended to reinforce difference rather than strengthen common humanity. Compassion was not readily apparent at Digswell, where volunteers spoke of the women in ways that indicated some knowledge of their circumstances but no empathy, and at times with frustration at their lack of responsiveness to Christianity.

Volunteers indicated a willingness to proactively love by volunteering at the classes, based on a genuine interest in others. Many attributes of love were noted among volunteers, although one volunteer at times patronized the women attending and tended to speak of her own life rather than getting to know them. This group prayed together before the service each week and prayer was mentioned often. In contrast to Swindon, this suggested a spiritual group identity, where volunteers viewed themselves as a team in mission. Prayer for others is classified here as an act of love but could also be viewed as indicative of a motivation for converts, as demonstrated by observations and comments from Nancy and Dave.

The commitment and faithfulness of volunteers to the club over many years was seen as a proactive form of intentional loving, as were cultural adaptations by volunteers, such as sensitivity to style of dress, a form of skill acquisition. Many instances of displays of interest in the migrant women were recorded, and volunteers at times reflected that they saw the women as individual personalities. Many instances of expressions of love were recorded, such as when Joy, a lawyer, gave legal advice to one woman. Kindness, among other fruit of the Spirit, was evidenced multiple times. Such acts of love tended to be only one-way—from volunteers to the migrant women. Volunteers failed to create mutual space for the migrant women to input into their lives. It also appeared situation-specific, as the migrant women were not celebrated during interviews. This may be indicative of a project mentality among some volunteers, where expressing love during sessions was aimed at conversion. Volunteers did not listen to the women's stories during sessions, a possible indication that relationships were based around volunteers as "givers" and the migrants as "receivers."

The volunteers wanted people to become Christians, and the consequent ministry in the community was linked to this desire, perhaps an indication that the initiative was classed as mission. It is not clear whether volunteers would have run the club purely as a community service, with no hope of gaining converts. Volunteers had occasionally engaged in social action, such as setting up a residents' group to improve housing standards.

Unfortunately, I noted that failures in loving were as apparent as displays of fruit of the Spirit. Most of these failures in loving were on the part of one person, and although aware of her temper, she seemed less self-aware of her patronizing behaviors and the extent to which she spoke about herself. The extent to which flaws detract from the impact of our loving is difficult to ascertain. Dave, the church minister, did not appear to challenge these behaviors, although he stated that he was generally aware of them. This is indicative of a low view of the importance of accountability, review, supervision, and reflective practice as a means of loving others. Supervision and group action/reflection were absent and would have been invaluable in helping the person understand, self-regulate, and adapt negative behaviors and would have empowered others to confront effectively.

The most noted motivation was the desire for conversions. Within a spiritual framework, motivations speak to and inspire an ability to express love. Volunteers spoke about God more readily than at Swindon, indicating motivations for service arising from faith. Reference to conversions was also indicative of motivations, as were several statements of theological reflection, such as Dave's explanation of the holistic and compassionate nature of Jesus' ministry, which he wanted to emulate. Lack of interest in the Eid celebrations that took place during fieldwork may have indicated a motivation that was only concerned with bringing something (i.e., God) to the estate residents rather than sharing in a mutual, spiritual learning experience. Motivational CQ was demonstrated when Janet stated that her motivations for volunteering were "to get experience and skills in networking with different backgrounds and different cultures."

Nancy spoke of being motivated to volunteer after seeing needs she believed she could meet, and both she and Janet spoke of being motivated by their enjoyment of serving at the club. Dave enjoyed and was energized by cross-cultural engagement generally. Volunteers were observed choosing to sit among people from other cultures during church services and seemed comfortably motivated to mix interculturally. Intentionality describes well the motivations of these volunteers. For example, Janet stated that "one purpose is to provide something for the ladies, a need they have . . . and also . . . try to get to know some of the ladies that go to the sewing group and try to build friendships with them and look for opportunities that might come up."

Skills were mostly high, although a lack of skills was apparent in some areas. This is the category in which most traits of CQ could be expected. The cultural knowledge of the volunteers was the most highly developed skill. However, a lack of self-awareness or a resigned, passive attitude towards known faults was by far the most frequent code in this category, and it is suggested that this had a negative impact, especially on education, formation, and reflective practice. Intentionality emerged strongly, particularly when volunteers saw themselves as creating opportunities for gospel proclamation through community outreach programs, such as the sewing club and the summer camp. Group reflection was again absent as a way of enabling volunteers to reflect on behaviors and intentions.

Numerous statements of theological belief and values were expressed and coded as skills, as the statements were based on a good working knowledge of theological frameworks. It is a skill to be able to apply knowledge of any kind to real-life situations. An ability to learn about culture from the African women was significant, as volunteers engaged their culture "on the job" and developed skills based on specific cross-cultural training. Volunteers showed higher thinking skills in their ability to process their motivations by applying them to reflections on their behaviors. It seemed that some of the building blocks of effective supervision were present but not utilized. All volunteers possessed the practical sewing skills necessary for helping the women who attended the group.

Volunteers possessed a far keener sense of being on mission than those at Swindon Baptist, a factor that seems to correlate with the high degree of intentionality. Volunteers spoke of "opportunities" arising during sessions and of "opportunities" to talk about life—including faith. Dave spoke of his frustration that almost no one among the African communities had become a Christian during the twenty years of estate ministry. Only Joy said that she did not consider the sewing club to be evangelistic. Even so, she often prayed out loud with different women and informally spoke about her Christian faith during sessions. Her stated aim was that of pastoral care, which included offering her professional skills to the residents. There was no clear, corporate, focused theological vision expressed.

Discussion about the Islamic faith of the estate residents and sharing about times when aspects of the Christian faith were shared with a wider group (e.g., the church camp) suggested an underlying hope that the estate residents would become Christians. Dave's interview disclosed relationship difficulties with some Muslims on the estate and he described the motivation of another local pastor, of a more liberal persuasion, as "anti-Christian." The otherness of estate residents seemed to be a dominating consideration for volunteers. Instead of attempting an interpathic understanding of their Islamic world, they sought to bring them over into their Christian culture. For instance, no consideration of joining in Eid celebrations or of interfaith dialogue was noted. Volunteers believed people needed to become Christians to obtain salvation, a perspective that appeared to drive their spiritual journeys and acted as a benchmark for success or failure in the church's outreach locally. This seemed to be held in tension with the belief that the work was God's, as demonstrated by the focus of group prayer before each church service and the reflections on faith shared during interviews.

A core narrative of conversionism was apparent from interviews and observations (church records were not kept) and provided significant motivation for all ministries of the estate congregation. These ministries included home tutoring, a homework club, a children's club, a workshop for mending household items for residents, the sewing club, and the family camp. The hope that these families would experience the love of God and become Christians was often referred to during interviews, exemplified by Joy's statement, "I just want them to experience him."

Both Dave and Nancy were trained in cross-cultural relating and had served as cross-cultural missionaries. Both stated that although they had known very little about Ethiopian and Sudanese cultures before working on the estate, they had read and learned from their experiences. Janet was currently a student training to work across different cultures. All volunteers displayed their growing understanding of these cultures through words and actions. For instance, Nancy stated that hospitality was not a high priority for these people, unlike other cultures in which she had lived. Dave spoke of the independent spirit of these previously nomadic people who had lived in very harsh conditions. Joy spoke of learning about Islam through numerous legal clients over the years. Nancy, Janet, and Joy all made respectful behavioral adaptations by dressing modestly among Muslim women, and Nancy and Joy mentioned the appropriateness of this during their interviews. Although Dave would usually come into the room during sessions, he did not engage in conversation with the women as he did not consider this appropriate. His knowledge and valuing of culture also emerged when he described and affirmed the Ethiopian and Sudanese residents as having a community approach to childcare and discipline, a view that extended to the children's club volunteers and to all church volunteers during the family camp.

Motivation for cross-cultural relating is a common domain of intercultural competence, including CQ.[3] Motivations for interacting cross-culturally correlated with participant desires for conversions. Dave stated that he was energized by cross-cultural interactions, and Joy wanted to help residents with legal and child-raising issues. Desire to serve and to be relevant and sensitive to culture was evident but not strongly affirmed by education and reflection. Again, there was little opportunity for enhancing existing skills or reflecting upon motivations.

Summary of Significant Themes at Digswell

It was only at Digswell that empathy did not emerge as a major factor. Here, the narrative was more often one of how "difficult" residents were and how resistant or even hostile they were to the gospel. Volunteers spoke readily

3. Livermore, *Cultural Intelligence*, 45–56.

about God and their theological beliefs. Prayer was mentioned and demonstrated on numerous occasions, suggesting a motivation of acting for and with God's empowerment. The motivation of desiring conversions was apparent at the club, where volunteers sought opportunities to share about their faith. This, however, hindered celebration of the women attendees as they were.

Intentionality was particularly noted. While intentionality may be an outworking of motivations, the ability to act intentionally is, of itself, a skill. Volunteers demonstrated their ability to learn "on the job" about the cultures represented by the African women. A lack of group reflection and supervision was noted as hindering the positive development of this initiative.

GOVAN CHURCH OF CHRIST: ENGLISH CLASSES

Bronte led the classes at Govan, assisted by Greta, Imogen, Christa, Anthea, Brenda, Alan, Lois, and Margaret. Gideon, the pastor, visited regularly and interacted with both students and volunteers. All but Imogen were mature aged, all were Caucasian, and Anthea and Christa were European migrants. Volunteers did not speak of faith together and were not motivated by evangelism, except for Gideon, who intentionally participated in intercultural outreach to engage in gospel proclamation. All volunteers were friendly and welcoming, creating a relaxed, hospitable atmosphere. Volunteers did not meet together or coordinate teaching.

Hospitality was enacted through friendliness and a relaxed, welcoming atmosphere. Students were treated as equals and tutors were generous with their time, perhaps an indication of genuine interest, which extended to practical helping acts. Compassion for students was expressed often during interviews. Private prayer for students was spoken of on several occasions, and two instances of prayer between students and the pastor were noted. Group prayer among tutors was absent. Higher-level thinking about love was indicated during interviews and observed in practice. Faith was integrated with practice, with one tutor noting that they were unable to distinguish the two in practice.

The most common motivation was enjoyment, which has similarities with the strong category of motivation based on an interest in people from other cultures. These codes may be indicative of a fit between calling and gifting, possibly resulting from an emphasis in church life on personal formation. A desire for gospel proclamation was strongly apparent, although almost all believed this meant demonstrating God's love-in-action rather than verbal proclamation during lessons.

The pastor's views about having evangelistic aims behind any church-based initiative were expressed by modeling outreach through interested engagement with attendees. Other volunteers did not appear to respond to his belief, however, appearing ambivalent about aims, while they were genuinely interested in their students and simply wanted to serve through teaching English. This was, however, linked to their faith, as noted above, and several considered that this activity might be a step in a journey towards conversion.

Skills were noted mainly in relation to teaching English. As with English classes at Swindon Baptist, the high skill levels of some tutors were offset by the low skills of others, suggesting that tutors were equipped to teach based on random life experiences, rather than purposeful education or training. For instance, some tutors were careful to modify their speech to the students, while others spoke rapidly. Some tutors were skilled at asking open questions, while others were not. Unexplained use of idioms was a common fault among tutors. Critical thinking skills were not particularly high among tutors and ongoing skill development opportunities were absent.

Levels of teaching skills varied, as did levels of intercultural competence. Group action/reflection sessions would have provided natural opportunities for group learning in these areas. Additionally, group work would have created opportunities to discuss and agree on the aims of the initiative and helped create a corporate spiritual identity among volunteers, creating a more unified approach to the initiative. None of this happened.

While the pastor taught and modeled mission, there was no clear connection between his approach and that of the volunteers. This may be indicative of systems not functioning within church life due to an emphasis on personal formation.

When asked during interviews, tutors were ambivalent about evangelism during or out of lessons. Bronte stated that she had started the classes purely to meet language and friendship needs among new migrants. Margaret also viewed the lessons as aiming to meet needs to learn English. Brenda did not believe that many students would attend the classes if evangelism happened during lessons and stated that friendship with the students was significant in itself, without evangelistic aims being included. Their attitudes contrasted with those of Gideon who wanted the lessons to have an underlying aim of evangelism. When asked about the purpose of the lessons, he replied that the purpose

> (A) is to build people's English. (B) is to build contacts from the church into people in the community . . . to bring them into church. . . . That's how I look at it. If you're just doing it for the sake of it, you're missing the point. . . . And Matthew 28, this is a stepping-stone to build a bridge to help us, to enable us to hopefully share with them the gospel.

Anthea also saw one purpose of the lessons as evangelistic. Whether or not Gideon's theology of mission was endorsed by the volunteers, the other tutors did not appear to have a formed idea as to how evangelism could happen through lessons. Being an evangelical congregation implied a commonly held belief that non-Christians need to respond positively to an encounter with Jesus to be granted salvation. Volunteers were not, however, asked to define evangelism at any fieldwork location. Expressed desires to serve the language needs of migrants, coupled with the lack of exploration as to how people might hear the gospel, seemed to create a degree of uncertainty about whether some of the tutors actually did believe this. For instance, Bronte, well-regarded by all tutors, was a highly educated woman who thoughtfully engaged her Christian faith. She did not consider the classes to be in any way evangelistic.

Individual Christian growth was identified as a core narrative at Govan. Searches through past bulletins dating back many years identified weekly devotions encouraging personal growth on the front page. This was never balanced with devotions about community life or, indeed, any other issue. The sermon at the service I attended also concerned personal spiritual growth. Several volunteers spoke of personal times of prayer for students, while corporate prayer was absent among volunteers. When asked about faith matters during interviews, volunteers spoke with ease, in contrast to those at Swindon. I did not hear or participate in any group conversations concerning faith.

As at Swindon Baptist, tutors possessed various levels of intercultural competency, seemingly dependent on past learning experiences and possibly their capacity for critical thinking. For instance, Greta routinely applied her knowledge of TEFL (Teaching English as a Foreign Language) to her lessons. Bronte moderated her speech when talking with students and displayed an interest in their countries of origin. Anthea had little previous contact with migrants, but this was mitigated by her gentle, friendly approach and her interest in others. Christa talked about her wartime experiences during lessons. Recounting the difficulties she had experienced in neutral Switzerland during the Second World War displayed low cultural sensitivity, as many students had arrived in Australia as refugees. She did, however, attempt to speak simple English in an emerging ability to modify her speech when relating cross-culturally.

Intercultural competencies were, therefore, somewhat inconsistent at Govan. Although Greta spoke of a need to improve these skills among tutors, this did not happen in practice. Again, education and training were absent, and the opportunity to learn from both individual and group experiences was lost.

Summary of Significant Themes at Govan

Relaxed interaction at classes complemented a simple desire to support students with compassion, care, and friendship in response to need, which was indicative of individual spiritual formation. This contrasted with the pastor's aim that every church-based initiative should be directly evangelistic. Volunteers were motivated to volunteer by their Christian faith and an interest in forming relationships with people from different cultures. Skill levels in teaching and in relating to students were also inconsistent, with instances of high and low skill levels being recorded in roughly equal measure. This may have been reflective of a considerable variance in levels of education among volunteers. As with the case at Swindon, this finding is probably indicative of skills not being taught to the volunteers at Govan.

Group prayer and planning sessions were absent. The lack of joint prayer and planning created a sense of volunteers working independently, with the only group cohesion coming through casual conversation. The emphasis on individual formation within church life may have worked to diminish group spirituality.

HOPE INTERNATIONAL / NORTHERN TRAINING: CHILD DAY CARE TRAINING SCHOOL

Thamina, the manager, oversaw the day-to-day running of the Registered Training Organization (RTO) at Northern Training. She was assisted by her team of teachers, known as trainers, Rhonda, Sally, Lilly, Jacinta, and Ellie. They shared a strong sense of mission, and all were motivated to empower new migrant women to find employment. All but one trainer had experienced migration, and most needed to retrain to access employment. The school management team shared a strong sense of Christian mission that sought to embody locally the good news of the reign of God. As manager, Thamina cared for her staff, a pastoral support from management that Rhonda and Jacinta (not church members) recognized and spoke of. Thamina's approach set the tone of care evident among staff and between staff and students. Lilly viewed her role as ministry rather than a job. Staff were all happy to be at Northern Training, and several declared they would not move, even if they could earn more money elsewhere. For Lilly, the team was "family" to her, a description that covered a shared sense of team and community.

Although the Christian trainers were clear that it was inappropriate to engage in gospel proclamation during classes due to government regulations, they readily spoke of God working in their lives. For instance, Lilly spontaneously described a dream she had about Thamina, believing that it was God-given and which Thamina received as such, reflecting a very personal aspect of spirituality. Trainers recounted how they had prayed with or for students. While at no point were the mostly Muslim students invited to church events, a sense of the immanence of God was witnessed to and apparent in the occasions cited above.

The passion of the staff may have reflected the passionate worship and preaching at services, where a sense of a powerful and immanent God was conveyed. Because most staff saw each other several times a week, there was a strong sense of family. Joy among staff was expressed, as was a high degree of practical and spiritual care for one another.

Most trainers and management were of South Asian origin. They were mostly empowering other South Asians from several cultures, plus a small minority of Anglo-Australian and Middle Eastern students. This reflected the profile of the local community, where a high proportion of residents came from the Indian subcontinent. A form of prophetic care was evident at Northern Training, where the school had been established to challenge the cultural and societal norms that led to new migrants struggling to find employment. Aspects of this were subversive, in that the difficulty in finding employment was subverted by learning new skills in the Australian context, leading to the employment of migrants. This was despite common racial bias in employment. The training school had recently been a finalist

PART 1

in local business awards, at which their prophetic message to Australia was displayed.

The love and care displayed among staff at Northern Training contributed to the caring atmosphere among trainers and students. Trainers felt supported by management, and in turn they supported the students. Non-Christian trainers reported that they felt cared for and supported by the Christian trainers and management and spoke very favorably of them. Trainers all expressed warmth, enthusiasm, and care through their words and in their focused attention to every student.

Weekly group prayer and intentional expressions of love for students and each other set a tone of community and purpose. Trainers reported minimal student attendance at church services or events. This did not seem to trouble them, for the aim was to empower and to care, not to evangelize. Prayer was reported occasionally between trainers and students, mainly as trainers responded to need. The effect of this approach at Northern Training cannot be quantified.

Perhaps the most striking contrast to other field locations was the ease with which trainers spoke of their faith. They were highly motivated to care for their students. Another contrast lay in the ambitious nature of this project. While the other initiatives were conducted on an amateur, volunteer basis, this community service required trained professionals and an adherence to government teaching standards. The following findings emerged from data collected during classes, interviews with staff and students, three church services, and a graduation ceremony.

Love was expressed often and in many ways by volunteers. Prayer was discussed, occurred among staff, and occasionally occurred with individual students. Christian staff spoke easily of their perceptions of God working in the training school and their responses to this. This was the only location studied where people outside the Christian faith worked alongside Christians, and they responded positively to experiences of receiving Christian love in many forms. Employing non-Christians indicated a belief that God will work through anyone for the good of others, a very inclusive stance. Trainers displayed loving attitudes to other staff, students, and the researcher in simple, practical ways that assisted the research process.

Love was often expressed practically and directly to students. In a friendly learning environment, trainers gave time and individual attention to students. Empathy was often evident, expressed for instance by trainers reassuring nervous students and giving emotional support. Trainers clearly wished to empower students in line with the rationale behind the training school. This enabled them to get to know one another well by using a down-to-earth manner with students and even confronting their behavior when appropriate. Students knew what trainers were thinking, while also knowing that they cared, enabling an open, honest environment that encouraged a deeper level of relationships. Retention rates among students were very high at Northern Training, no doubt due to the hospitable community formed by the trainers who made themselves available to the students.

Many positive intrinsic motivations were noted, especially the desire to empower students. Motivations stemming from Christian faith were common, including a sense of vocation on the part of trainers. Extrinsic motivations for one trainer focused on money, while, for another, financial success was linked to having God's favor. Trainers recounted, and were observed persevering in, some very difficult circumstances. This was indicative of motivations fostered by a sense of vision and calling.

Attitudes and actions in establishing and running the RTO included prayer, vision, perseverance, and a desire to stay within God's will. Many comments and actions indicated the motivations of staff towards students and other staff. This included paying the staff well and the observation that the RTO leadership had been instrumental in establishing the culture of the organization. Other statements indicated that motivations were inspired by Christian faith among staff, including their commitment to professionalism and the success of the RTO. Outcomes were clearly linked to staff being obedient to what they believed God was telling them.

Good teaching skills were common, although poorer teaching skills were also apparent. Some poorer skills were a result of trainers teaching in a second language, and extra training and support were warranted. Continuous improvement through reflection and group supervision was absent, as was one-on-one monitoring. This was possibly a management blind spot, as Thamina spoke of the intentionality of management in producing excellence. Lilly periodically offered professional development sessions to other trainers, although not during fieldwork. Some building blocks of ongoing formation were apparent but not capitalized upon. Unsurprisingly, trainers had a strong awareness of cultural difference, as all but Lilly were themselves migrants. This probably resulted in the high levels of empathy noted.

All Christian trainers described a sense of being called to their role, which may be viewed as a sense of being on mission. Talk about operating within the will of God was frequent and of the three non-Christian trainers interviewed, two also strongly indicated a sense of vocation in teaching, a value that was an active part of the culture and environment for all. Each trainer understood that, in accordance with government regulations, they could not evangelize during class. None stated that they had a problem with this restriction. All Christian trainers offered to pray with or for students, and prayer emerged as an important factor in practice and theory.

Trainers believed that this initiative was motivated by a desire to provide a needed service for the local population, rather than by a desire for converts. One trainer did consider the RTO to have an evangelistic role but did not overtly proselytize. Trainers were also very aware of the pluralistic context in which they were teaching and were very respectful of student beliefs. The desire to respond to need in the neighborhood suggested a theology of mission towards the local community, as well as towards international ministries.

Hope International Church likes to think big. Thamina believed the senior pastor wanted the RTO to become the biggest employer in the municipality. At that time, the church had a staff of around twenty and a large congregation of well over two thousand regular attendees. The church also assisted congregations overseas. Big thinking and the desire to serve the needs of migrants aligned with the inaugural aims of the RTO.

An important development in Pentecostalism has been the understanding that mission should include social welfare.[4] The RTO was closely aligned to this belief, and it is of particular interest that Christian volunteers passionately sought to do this and did not seek converts, content to be bound, through being an accredited agency, by the prohibition on proselytizing. This hardly seemed to matter, as the love offered was passionate, committed, and joyful.

A theology that correlated success with numerical growth within church life may explain a tendency to exaggerate, as when trainers stated that students had become Christians but, when pressed, could not give further details about this. At the graduation ceremony, one of the pastors stated publicly that the RTO had come second in the local business awards. In fact, there was one winner with all other entrants classed as runners-up. A pastor's observation that the church's multicultural pastor was "ahead of his time" for initiating intercultural outreach projects was open to challenge given the numerous multicultural pastors throughout Australia. Perhaps

---

4. Clifton, *Pentecostal Churches in Transition*, 165.

these incidents resulted from the positivity that permeated all aspects of church life and motivated members.

Participants were clearly formed by three core narratives: thinking big, passionate faith, and seeking to care for the local community. These were marks of the RTO, which closely aligned core narratives and expressions of care.

Most trainers were recent migrants from the Indian subcontinent, several speaking English as a second language. Teaching styles revealed a fusion of cultural styles from their countries of origin. Trainers often spoke rapidly without modifying speech, despite one trainer saying that her students often failed to understand her lessons. One field note entry states that "I [the researcher] had to concentrate to understand her accent and rapid speech." However, notwithstanding these obvious areas for improvement, all trainers appreciated the difficulties faced by migrant students and understood the cultural expectations of their daily lives.

Significant Emerging Themes at Northern Training

Love was expressed in many and varied ways at Northern Training. Spirituality was expressed overtly by the Christian trainers, and this was referred to positively by those of other faiths. Regular corporate prayer and talk about prayer characterized staff. Within the warm, friendly, and welcoming environment of the RTO, humility towards both students and researcher was demonstrated by trainers.

A marked asset of the RTO was the individual attention given to students, reflecting trainers' desires for student success and their desire to empower. Focused attention was reminiscent of several tutors at Swindon Baptist who saw their students as individuals rather than just a cohort. The RTO was founded out of a desire for the church to serve identified needs within the local community. This resulted in the desire to empower students, born out of empathy, a significant intrinsic motivation for trainers.

Hard work, self-belief, and trust in God's goodness in establishing and running Northern Training were noted and spoke clearly of motivations of the management who created the RTO. All trainers spoke of their enjoyment working in this team, a genuine response to the commitment of management to the well-being of staff.

Perhaps the most striking contrast to other field locations was the sense of God's immanence, often expressed during conversations. They were highly motivated to care for their students. Another contrast lay in the ambitious nature of this project. While the other initiatives were conducted on an amateur, volunteer basis, this community service required trained professionals and an adherence to government teaching standards.

The following short chapter will summarize the major findings from this study and introduce major themes to be explored in the remainder of this book.

QUESTIONS FOR REFLECTION AND DISCUSSION

- If you are part of an intercultural initiative, how is love of God and neighbor expressed?
- Can you identify themes that influence how your initiative is run? For example, you might realize that everything happens on the run, rather than being planned and prayed for.

5

Major Emerging Themes
Planning and Practicing Intercultural Pastoral Care

Joy often prayed short prayers out loud during the sewing club. Sometimes it was for the sewing equipment to work, and once she laid her hand on the belly of a pregnant woman and prayed for her baby. I wondered what the Muslim women thought about these prayers. Did they appreciate them, ignore them, or resent them?

MAJOR FINDINGS EMERGED FROM the data. These will form the basis of discussion in part 2. I concluded that church-based, intercultural initiatives will most effectively communicate love of God and neighbor when organization and delivery follow the principles, practices, and functions of intercultural pastoral care.

Attributes of intercultural pastoral care were expressed either positively or negatively at the four initiatives. Skills noted were either indications of intercultural competence or were specific to each initiative. For instance, teaching English was a skill specific to Swindon and Govan.

These still fit within the framework for intercultural pastoral care, an aspect of which is that when activities take place as a means of expressing care, pastoral care that enables and empowers occurs. Skills might also be considered as an additional resource for pastoral care. Skills for pastoral care, mission, or both together were inconsistent, probably due to a lack of training, group reflection, and planning. Inconsistency in intercultural competence was also apparent, and consistently higher levels would have strengthened practice and expressions of love. Pastors who engage in systems thinking throughout church life usually proactively address issues arising at initiatives and feed this into ongoing training and reflection through group engagement, home groups, church-wide prayer meetings, and sermons. This did not happen.

Numerous other, minor themes identified in the data fit well within the scope of intercultural pastoral care. Spirituality for pastoral care was one area of care absent to different degrees at Swindon and Govan. While the four initiatives might be classed as mission, this paradigm did not account for all the data.

The efficacy of church-based, intercultural initiatives in demonstrating love of God and neighbor will be greatly enhanced when volunteers attend to their ability to express love through their motivations for participating and when they consistently seek to improve the skills required for the service they are providing. This includes learning intercultural competencies. This statement indicates three areas that require ongoing attention for effective intercultural pastoral care to take place: expressions of love, motivations, and skills. While church-based groups might choose to organize their life and practice around critical pastoral thinking, this breakdown into three categories is an easy and efficient way of thinking about what is required and is, therefore, more accessible for volunteers.

Mission planning and practice should always be informed by the foundational elements of pastoral care. Participants who effectively displayed love of God and neighbor did so by applying, perhaps unconsciously, elements of pastoral care practice. This was particularly evident at Northern Training where participants attended to students' emotional, spiritual, and practical needs. Empathy shown at all locations enabled communication of love. Expressions of love was the largest and most complex category to emerge from coding. Empathy and compassion are rich pastoral themes that were indicated strongly from data at three locations. They were expressed within the initiatives, during interviews, and, at times, following sessions. This was evident through a hospitable community atmosphere where mutually enriching friendships could be birthed and diversity could be celebrated. Conversion agendas and low intercultural competence

MAJOR EMERGING THEMES

prevented genuine mutuality at times and detracted from deepening expressions of love.

Theological formation and theological reflection are required to understand the distinctive boundaries between pastoral care, community development, welfare support, and advocacy in relation to evangelism. Pastoral care is mission, and mission is pastoral care.

I discovered that core church narratives directly impact the aims and conduct of church-based, intercultural initiatives. Direct links between core church narratives and participant beliefs and behaviors were noted at all locations.

Models of intercultural competence, including Cultural Intelligence (CQ), did not account for or influence participant ability to express love of God and neighbor. Loving behaviors could be attributed to numerous factors not connected to intercultural competence: empathy, compassion, a desire to serve in church life, and personal formation (or a lack of this). There was crossover with intercultural competence, for instance, when self-awareness played a role in abilities to express love, but the model is of limited help in forming volunteers for loving service to others.

Other strong trends were identified from the data, which, while having insufficient evidence to be designated as theory, are still worth careful consideration. I found that individualism inhibits or prevents successful communication of love of God and neighbor, group cohesion, and the sharing of aims. I define individualism here as volunteers looking to their own ideas and interests rather than primarily viewing themselves as team members together in service. Individualism was noted at Swindon Baptist and Govan Church of Christ. At these locations volunteers did not share a common purpose of care for migrants and did not coordinate teaching or care. This did not afford migrants opportunities to experience Christian community. Individualism also resulted in poor coordination of lessons, and, due to a lack of skill-sharing or team spirit, created an uneven level of teaching skill at Swindon and Govan. The intentionality particularly noted at Digswell was absent at Swindon and Govan.

Spirituality needs nurturing in individuals and groups for volunteers to better express love of God and neighbor. Volunteers need enabling to speak about their spiritual journeys if evangelism is ever, in any context, to be effective. This would enable a formed and nurtured spirituality and theology, rather than the random theologies (with little shared discussion or exploration) of volunteers found at Swindon and Govan. A more uniform theology of the initiatives was found at Digswell and Northern Training, where group spirituality was nurtured. Elements of the fruit of the Spirit were apparent at all locations, even if occasionally compromised by negative behaviors. It was not, however, always clear whether this was a result of a nurtured spirituality. A desire to offer empowerment was commonly expressed, resonating with the functions of pastoral care.

The activism of evangelicalism can subsume the pursuit of team-based spirituality and pastoral care formation at church-based initiatives. The studies of Swindon and Govan may indicate that, while congregants are willing and in some cases feel obliged to offer their time in providing a service to people outside the church, this did not appear to extend to a willingness to spend time in joint spiritual nurture and reflection. Further studies might seek more evidence for this hypothesis, which was not confirmed at Digswell or Northern Training.

A spirituality of care and principles of practice, therefore, need to be nurtured among volunteers. Such initiatives risk not thriving without theological education, spiritual formation, supervision, training, and professional development, and will be impoverished without a constant process of review in the context and culture of service. Learning goals should align with healthy core narratives and clear mission strategy.

Where spirituality was nurtured by volunteers this was reflected in their words and actions during initiatives and during interviews. In some cases, this was an individual journey that hindered a sense of group identity and resulted in a lack of prayer, planning, and reflection together. This was apparent in the manner of relating between volunteers. For instance, group spirituality at Northern Training created a sense of unity and a sense of connection between faith and service that was difficult to discern at Swindon. Numerous volunteers were motivated by a sense of satisfaction and vocation, although this did not always correspond with statements regarding God-inspired service, a strong theme for others.

Motivations strongly affect the way initiatives are conducted, and enjoyment and satisfaction may be stronger motivations than faith for volunteers at church-based initiatives. This would be true of both intercultural and monocultural initiatives. Enjoyment as a motivation is viewed as positive when it aligns giftings with calling. A primary aim of the initiative at Digswell was conversion, and this was seen as limiting volunteers' abilities to celebrate the women attending as they were. Framing church-based, intercultural initiatives primarily as vehicles for evangelism can, therefore, confuse and compromise the ability of volunteers to express love.

The goals of evangelism will be achieved as volunteers engage in pastoral care. Inclusive communities, in which Christians live and love alongside non-Christians in a mutuality of care, can act as vehicles for discipleship and as invitations to faith for non-Christians.[1] Evangelism was a strong motivation at Digswell and appeared directly related to a theology that considered all who do not become Christians to be "destined for hell," to use their terms. There was a general sense of playing into an undefined sense of evangelism at other initiatives, although no bridges into programs such as Alpha or other church events were offered, except for occasional invitations to special services. Evangelism was not a motivation for many who believed initiatives should be no more than hospitality and empowering for members of the community.

The following chapters will explore how an intercultural pastoral care framework might strengthen expressions of love of God and neighbor at church-based, intercultural initiatives. As noted earlier, most discussion subjects have application well beyond the limits of this study and might be applied to any church-based community initiative and to any mission endeavors.

QUESTION FOR REFLECTION AND DISCUSSION

- Which themes identified in this chapter align, either positively or negatively, with your church initiative?

---

1. Stone, *Evangelism after Christendom*.

PART 2

6

Functions of Pastoral Care

The end of term party at Swindon was a fun-filled occasion. In addition to eating wonderful food, games were played, which became noisy and competitive. Most people laughed often, and inhibitions were shed. This may have been a form of healing for some or nurture for others—an opportunity to de-stress from the challenges of navigating life as a new migrant. Laughter bonds people and was perhaps indicative of nascent friendships that would heal and sustain over many years.

FOR DECADES WE HAVE been told the central work of the church is preaching, mission, and growth. While more recently the growth mentality has been seriously questioned, pastoral care still tends to be a peripheral activity. Yet pastoral care, properly understood, is simply loving others well. This is not limited to the congregation but should emanate out into the community and much further, through our advocacy and financial aid for those around the world who are suffering. The thesis of this book is that pastoral care practices are in reality a form of mission, while also having an intrinsic value.

An early definition of the functions of pastoral care by Clebsch and Jaekle was limited to healing, sustaining, guiding, and reconciling.[1] Other "helping acts" they believed were beyond the scope of pastoral care. This

---

1. Clebsch and Jaekle, *Pastoral Care in Historical Context*, 4.

PART 2

limited definition still appears to be the understanding of many in the churches. This narrow approach to care has long been superseded by Clinebell, Lartey, and others, who have identified the functions of pastoral care as healing, sustaining, guiding, nurturing, empowering, reconciling, and liberating. Lartey includes prophetic care on this list, a function similar to liberating.

The four congregations studied all expressed some of these functions. Jean, at Swindon, nurtured by inviting her students to share Christmas with her family. The sewing club empowered women to make their culturally appropriate garments. Teaching English to migrants at both Swindon and Govan was a form of liberating. Students at Northern Training were nurtured and empowered by the care and attention of their trainers.

In this chapter I will explore each of these functions and will demonstrate how each can be a missional expression of the love of God. My discussion of the functions is not exhaustive but will demonstrate that the functions of pastoral care are vital for noncoercive mission.

HEALING

Jesus healed physically, as testified in the Gospels and Acts, but he also came to heal the brokenhearted (Luke 4:18). Many in our congregations, including ourselves, have been brokenhearted. Healing in the church comes in many forms—inclusion in the life of the church, faithful friendships, being listened to and affirmed, and simply having fun together. Prayer, with and for others, helps bind broken hearts, as does hearing and receiving God's message of hope. It is in the healing acts of Christians that the truth of this message is revealed.

When congregations include outsiders in the wider life of the church, the likelihood of healing is enhanced. This inclusion makes available healing acts of listening and affirming friendships and offers the possibility of reciprocal relationships. This healing through friendship can take place in any setting, in or far from the church.

Healing is offered at any church-based initiative where restoration is available, be it spiritual, psychological, or emotional, even if healing is not considered a primary aim.[2] The English conversation classes in this study offered new migrants an opportunity to come to know locals and become better equipped to function in society. This offered a measure of healing

2. Lartey, *In Living Color*, 62.

FUNCTIONS OF PASTORAL CARE

from the sense of estrangement so often experienced by migrants, that erosive isolation and disenfranchisement that cries out for emotional, psychological, and spiritual restoration. This is important as many migrants have lost rich community. The altruism of volunteers, in contrast to the many salaried (albeit kind) functionaries that migrants deal with daily, carries a healing message of love and inclusion, as evidenced by volunteers.

Participants engaged with migrants as caregivers, requiring active listening and empathic responding.[3] They did not view their activities as healing. A realization of this connection through theological reflection could be a strong motivator for volunteers to explore ways in which this function might be enhanced. Some participants were empathetic listeners, an important skill for active listening that requires emotional commitment to be actively sensitive to the speaker's emotional needs. This requires information to be processed through understanding and remembering what is said and responding through verbal and nonverbal communication.[4]

Reciprocity in relationships is vital for healing as it respects the self-worth of the other. Recognizing the gifts others have to offer us can be healing for those who have been marginalized and devalued. Some of us raised in evangelical circles have been taught that those outside the church are to be feared for their corrupt influence, and mission methods have implied this, teaching proclamation that does not simultaneously listen to the voices of others. Where people are loved and affirmed, when they are given a voice, they experience a measure of healing, and we can learn from their wisdom and experience. This is mission, even if we are never invited to offer the reason for our hope (1 Pet 3:15).

My research indicated that healing was less likely where Christians at church-based initiatives had an overriding conversion agenda, such as at Digswell. Instead of offering gifts of healing, the migrants attending the sewing club were described as "difficult" or "resistant" for their perceived failure to demonstrate an interest in Christianity. In other instances, healing took place in some measure. Churches offering English conversation classes to new migrants offered community to those with little English, an antidote to loneliness. The volunteer nature of the classes spoke of genuine care, and friendships were enabled to various degrees, largely dependent on volunteers' ability to continue relationship building outside lesson times. These volunteers told me they were inspired by these newcomers, most of

3. Clinebell and McKeever, *Basic Types of Pastoral Care*, 70.
4. Manzano et al., "Active Listening."

whom were far from loved ones because they had to flee their countries or were seeking better outcomes for their children in Australia.

SUSTAINING

Community plays an important role in sustaining us all. We are created to be social beings, and without several meaningful encounters each week, most of us are unable to thrive. I find sustenance in my church community. I am sustained by church attendance through the worship, prayer, and preaching. Meeting friends and welcoming newcomers brings joy and frames my week, Sunday to Sunday. Meals and outings and other fun times together cement these friendships and afford opportunities for deeper sharing and listening.

Sustaining runs deeper too. In times of crisis, I have needed the sustenance afforded by close friendships. Remembering our own needs for sustenance can create empathy for the suffering of others. Offering sustenance to those outside the church is vital to our calling as Christians. This may include anyone with whom we have contact. For instance, many in our churches regularly work alongside others who have rarely, if ever, encountered Christian friendship. As Christ-followers we are called to love others by offering sustenance through difficult times. Kind words, careful listening, expressions of empathy, meals, and other practical help all express God's love. These are to be freely given, expecting no reciprocity or presupposed outcome.

Sustaining is helping others endure suffering in which restoration or healing seems either unlikely or impossible.[5] Volunteers played a sustaining role for attendees through offers of friendship and practical assistance. This special gift came to many whose roots and communities of meaning had been left behind in their home country and for whom trauma is individually and corporately ever-present in its effects. A "theology of presence" is relevant to those moments when an intercultural carer offers care. When we discover other cultures, we learn that what we understood to be reality is in fact only our interpretation of realities, which we only perceive in part. We start to understand that many things we thought to be universal are in fact the perceptions of our culture, many things we considered absolutes are relative, and what we considered simple is in fact complex.[6]

5. Clebsch and Jaekle, *Pastoral Care in Historical Perspective*, 8–9.
6. Augsburger, *Pastoral Counseling*, 18.

The interpathic ability and willingness to bracket one's own worldview and step carefully and observingly into the world of the other is a significant factor in providing sustaining care that becomes consistent companioning in a complex, multicultural context. As volunteers begin to step into a place between cultures and develop some degree of relationship with migrants, they may be able to encourage them on this reciprocal, community-building journey. Recognizing cultural values as relative, without being pressured to abandon them, becomes a sustaining activity that can break down the sense of cultural isolation often experienced by migrants. As pastoral carers journey with migrants, companioning them in lessons, workshops, or sewing sessions, they provide care that sustains migrants in their new and alien environment.

Where motivations are to sustain, the necessary learning has formational requirements such as laying aside personal agendas, developing interpersonal relating skills, and gaining cultural knowledge. What level of commitment to additional learning and training can reasonably be expected of volunteers? Where pastors personally model these values and behaviors and create a supporting culture, others might learn more readily through action/reflection sessions during which modeled behaviors are explained. Care offered only within the time span of sessions can be experienced as sustaining care over time, although time spent together outside initiatives is likely to accelerate and enrich relationship building.

While the giving of sustenance was noted at the initiatives, it was only an intentional group commitment at Northern Training, where trainers gave whatever support was needed for successful student outcomes. Such was their commitment to this that trainers had been known to respond to texts received late at night from students experiencing domestic conflict or requesting prayer. The freedom students felt to do this suggests that the message of care and support had been enacted through demonstrations of support during contact hours. Sandy, Jean, and Karen were noted as offering sustaining care at Swindon, but this was on their initiative rather than an agreed group practice, reliant on emotional intelligence and a personal commitment to care.

PART 2

GUIDING

The giving of spiritual guidance has been an aspect of pastoral care in every age.[7] Guidance can be defined as supporting problem-solving, skill development, or decision-making to help others draw out their latent abilities through our loving concern and faith in God.[8] This might also include drawing out potential that will empower the individual and could include challenge and gentle confrontation, enabling others to appreciate their God-given possibilities—spiritually, psychologically, and morally.[9] This mature response of encouraging adult learning emerged at all sites, albeit in embryonic ways. Volunteers helped students navigate life situations by finding their own inner resources, which was also observed frequently between trainers and students at Northern Training. This enabling guidance was offered to migrants through the educative elements of training, mentoring, and information support.

Guidance at Northern Training was offered as students were helped to enter the workplace to use their innate and developed skills. When trainers listened to students share about their lives and asked clarifying questions,[10] this indicated the importance of training in educative guidance (reframing, paraphrasing and summarizing, questioning and probing, etc.). Participatory sense making involves two persons working together towards meaning making.[11] This process might be applied to processes of educative guidance. Those who have power in any form may be tempted to offer inductive guidance. This happens when the care seeker is encouraged to make decisions using the values and criteria of the caregiver.[12] Inductive guidance was not observed at any location, or reported by volunteers, indicating a high level of respect for the autonomy of attendees.[13]

While volunteers may be friends rather than mentors, we should not seek to mentor others if we ourselves are lost.[14] This applies to volunteers offering guidance and indicates the importance of nurturing spirituality

---

7. Pembroke, *Art of Listening*, 10n14.
8. Lartey, *In Living Color*, 64.
9. Pembroke, *Art of Listening*, 1-10.
10. Clebsch and Jaekle, *Pastoral Care in Historical Perspective*, 9.
11. Pembroke, *Foundations for Pastoral Counseling*, ch. 2.
12. Clebsch and Jaekle, *Pastoral Care in Historical Perspective*, 9.
13. Clebsch and Jaekle, *Pastoral Care in Historical Perspective*, 9.
14. Robinson, *Soul Mentoring*, 4.

and supervision. Intercultural competence, especially cultural knowledge, informs pastoral carers as to whether and how guidance is appropriate in a cross-cultural relationship. For instance, teachers are held in high regard in Confucian cultures where rote learning is common. Students familiar with teachers telling them what to think may assume this posture automatically. Understanding these differences enables tutors to adapt to students.

Guiding requires deep listening as presenting issues are often underlaid by a deeper meaning. Being a listener who acts as a sounding board is pastoral care that might additionally be mission. Offering guidance in this manner demonstrates the love of God and is a component of communicating God's love. It is God who sovereignly watches over the lives of us all, and we are called proactively to cooperate with God by proclaiming his love through our conduct.

There are preconditions for offering guidance in a pastoral care setting. While trust is to some degree conferred on a counselor in a formal setting, pastoral care takes place more spontaneously. Most of us need good reason for trusting someone for guidance. This requires having spent time with them and seeing how they interact with others around them. Do they listen to others? Do their words sound wise and non-reactionary? Are they in love with their own voice or do they signal value and respect for others' opinions? Guidance as pastoral care and mission requires a context and opportunity for the building of reciprocal friendships. Our love of programs in the church has potential to help or hinder in this respect. Church-based initiatives are insufficient by themselves for building close relationships unless they have continued for long periods of time.

Some at the initiatives demonstrated the potential for offering guidance. Jean at Swindon was a patient listener who extended classroom relationships and met her students outside the lesson times, including inviting them to share Christmas with her family. Sandy had helped her class of struggling students over the years with practical tasks such as making hospital appointments. The longevity of relationships, her willingness to help, and her obvious affection for students, noted during sessions, created the environment in which guidance might be sought. The group culture of care fostered at Northern Training offered opportunities for guidance. This may have been helped by cultural differences by which young South Asian brides, with no wider Australian family, looked up to their slightly older trainers as mother figures. Opportunities for guidance, as explained above, might have been possible if a group culture of care had been agreed to and

PART 2

fostered at the other initiatives. A vague understanding of the aims of initiatives and, at times, impoverished group cultures rendered this unlikely.

RECONCILING

One form of reconciliation in the classic pastoral tradition addresses the multifaceted process of forgiveness, while the other embodies a stance that involves "placing alienated persons into situations in which good relationships might be re-established."[15] This second form applies to all four projects.

Cultural divisions are often marked in Australian society, and different ethnicities can tend towards socializing within the same social grouping, often in specific geographic locations. Mistrust and racism still confront migrants, so, for many initiative attendees, the programs offered a safe, nonjudgmental environment where a level of reconciliation and good relationships within society were possible in the wider context of alienation. The importance of this for the cohesion of society should not be underestimated.

Although participants perhaps did not acknowledge or understand the important role they might play in modeling, initiating, and incarnating reconciliation at this level, the scope for this was significant. Asylum seekers, immigration, and racial tensions present significant challenges in Western societies. In the early days of the study, Sudanese gangs were often targeted by media and politicians alike, who portrayed the Sudanese as "problem migrants."[16] At the time of writing, the influence of Chinese migrants in Australian politics had become a point of political and economic conflict and discrimination.[17] Whatever the extent of these issues, they resulted in societal distrust and the othering of all migrants, even beyond ethnicity. Where healthy, mutual relationships are formed between nationals and any migrants, the general distrust of all people of these ethnicities is challenged. These relationships are a political statements and ones which the church has potential to model to society. The church is capable of both modeling love of the other while making a powerful political statement of embrace, inclusion, and valuing, an inherent message of reconciliation. What was achieved at the initiatives could be so much more significant if

15. Clebsch and Jaekle, *Pastoral Care in Historical Perspective*, 9.
16. Henriques-Gomes, "South Sudanese-Australians Report Racial Abuse."
17. Wade, "Australia-China Relations."

volunteers understood this role and the pastoral theological implications (an education and formation topic) of this high calling, which can have a significant impact on Australian society.

It is not possible to measure or quantify how much this level of reconciling permeated the relationships between volunteers and the African women at Digswell, but it should have been possible even with the existing research design. Differences in religion were evident of course, especially when articulated in front of each other. At this site, volunteers seemed less interested in reconciliation between people of different religions than in communicating the gospel, not realizing that this is in fact part of the gospel. This can compromise the gospel message of love of neighbor and maintain the power imbalance between volunteers and the women. This negative evaluation serves as a reminder that reconciliation in this sense is a formational and pastoral goal with clear societal value. In situations such as this, there exists a tension between mission and pastoral care that calls, in practical terms, for loving discernment and, in strategic terms, for pastoral and theological reflection.

The desire to communicate the gospel should not, however, be dismissed as inevitably working against reconciliation. The *missio Dei* is that of God's sending love, sent to reconcile all things and all peoples to God.[18] Incarnational living is powerful in this sense, as it demonstrates the love and acceptance of others modeled by Jesus.[19] This potentially results in reconciliation between people and with God. Clebsch and Jaekle include reconciliation with God in their definition of reconciliation as a pastoral function,[20] adding that it is intended to also bring reconciliation to communities.[21] However, the gospel promises to bring division. Jesus warned that his message would divide families against each other (Luke 12:51–53), a shocking message in first-century Palestinian culture where families viewed themselves as indivisible units. This would have also been the case for African families living on the estate, and an appreciation of this dynamic for the volunteers at Digswell would have contextualized some of the difficulties of residents responding to the gospel. This fertile ground for theological reflection and transformational practice was not just overlooked but was invisible.

18. Bosch, *Transforming Mission*, 10.
19. Frost and Hirsch, *Shaping of Things to Come*, 33–59.
20. Clebsch and Jaekle, *Pastoral Care in Historical Perspective*, 9.
21. Colley, "Community Approach to Overcoming Violence."

PART 2

To the extent that the Muslim community discovered that communication of the gospel was the aim of those at Digswell, divisions could have emerged, as the community was known to be internally policed by Muslim elders, some of whom were Islamists. This potential challenge highlights another tension between mission and pastoral care because it seems uncaring (and a severe challenge to any concept of reconciliation) to expect someone to break from family to live openly as a Christian. Some mission theory attempts to accommodate this problem by encouraging Islamic converts to view themselves as "Muslim Christians."[22] While this model is unacceptable to other missiologists,[23] this approach engages realistically with the immense pressures felt by Muslim converts to Christianity, a situation which demands a pastoral response to conversion. Pastoral caring should never be disconnected from mission, however that connection may be understood. The mission of God, and, indeed, God's very essence, is that of love and reconciliation. Konz argues that mission should not be based on "expedience and 'impact'" but rather on an understanding of the *missio Dei*, placing primacy on God's agency as reconciler of humankind.[24] Mission is never more important than love, which seeks to discern what response is appropriate at any given time. Love is the foundation for pastoral care and the foundation for mission. Pembroke places the foundation of pastoral care in the Trinity (which, by nature, is loving), arguing "positive relational dynamics in pastoral encounters can be viewed as mirroring the inner life of God."[25] The emphasis of the Lausanne Commitment on love may still challenge some cross-cultural missions literature, but it is a major theme of missional church literature, which emphasizes the importance of incarnational living.[26] The early church contextualized the gospel through incarnational living, which became its missional focus.[27] It can be difficult to find missions literature that prioritizes and develops themes of interpersonal relating skills in ways equally relevant to pastoral care. This seems a significant oversight, perhaps based on theory or theological exploration rather than implications for actual, on-the-ground, relational practice. David Livermore perhaps comes the closest to doing this in his discussion of

22. Travis, "C1 to C6 Spectrum," 407–8.
23. See Williams, "Revisiting the C1–C6 Spectrum."
24. Konz, "Even Greater Commission," 335.
25. Pembroke, *Renewing Pastoral Practice*, 7.
26. "Cape Town Commitment."
27. Wade, "Emerging Church."

CQ for short-term, cross-cultural missions when he relates growth in CQ to effectiveness in short-term missions.[28]

NURTURING

Nurturing care seeks to help others discover and develop giftings for the rest of their lives.[29] "Embodied listening" is a way of listening that moves into joint meaning making where questions of values, beliefs, and spiritual practices are raised that are important to seekers.[30] This provides a nurturing environment in which care seekers can tap into their inner resources with support, encouragement, and companioning.

Nurture of the whole person was a strong distinctive at all four initiatives, even though initially the focus was on the provision of services. The extent to which attendees were nurtured emotionally or spiritually depended on the volunteers they encountered. One person might be gifted pastorally and, therefore, loved, accepted, and enabled students, and another might speak of the different learning needs he perceived in his students and the ways in which he attempted to meet them. One offered appropriate legal services as a lawyer, her care for the person being relevant to her qualifications. When caring for others is a joy because the requisite skills fit well with our gifting, this nurturing approach generates greater patience, perseverance, and satisfaction, a pastoral stance which reflects the love of God. This tone is set through being aware of oneself and one's experiences.[31] This balanced blend of gift and joy naturally nurtures both giver and receiver and creates the presence necessary for the provision of pastoral care.[32] God's nurturing presence is mediated through the carer's own experience of nurture, and the carer represents and brings more than their own self because what the carer brings into a relationship is what care seekers can view as God's care.[33]

Spiritual nurture was identified at Northern Training through prayer with and for students and through the pastoral involvement of trainers in the lives of their students through hospitality. Nurture was present at the

28. Livermore, *Cultural Intelligence*, 27.
29. Clinebell and McKeever, *Basic Types of Pastoral Care*, 41.
30. Doehring, *Practice of Pastoral Care*, 64.
31. Patton, *Pastoral Care*, 24.
32. Patton, *Pastoral Care*, 25.
33. Patton, *Pastoral Care*, 25.

other three initiatives as volunteers prayed for migrants, sought to meet spiritual needs through relational connections, and offered practical or language skills. Each participant offered different modes of care, but the team aggregate added up to pastoral nurturing. The provision of a nurturing environment is important for migrants adjusting to living in a new country. Migrants react in different ways to living in a new culture. These range from self-confident adjustment to retreatism/avoidance and aggression towards the host culture.[34] Opportunities to build relationships, and the reality of experiencing them with other Australians, are instrumental in helping migrants in the second and third of these responses.

An important way in which church-based volunteers can nurture recent arrivals is by networking with care agencies—so, once again, referral skills are important. Nurture through competent referral may be an underestimated skill in pastoral ministry but never underestimated in pastoral counseling or professional spiritual care. It is important for volunteers (and pastors) to appreciate their limitations given that many asylum seekers are deeply traumatized. Christians can offer practical support and friendship, but attempts to counsel or act as amateur psychologists can be avoided by teaching referral skills to all pastoral workers. Pastoral carers in the context of the four projects were not counselors, although additional training in basic counseling skills might be viewed as an extension of existing skills in pastoral care.

Pastoral care and counseling are, therefore, separate but closely linked disciplines that can model best practice for workers in cross-cultural mission. There are certainly spiritual and qualitative aspects in common that nurture and care for persons, and while formal practice or boundaries between volunteers and professionals should not be blurred, there are common skills to be learned.

LIBERATION, EMPOWERMENT, ADVOCACY, AND PROPHETIC CARE

Some of the challenges that faced participants were born in the previous life experience of migrants, given that their beliefs may have been suppressed through threats, intimidation, coercion, or marginalization.[35] Therefore, a first step in liberation is often to support others as they free themselves

34. Arbuckle, *Earthing the Gospel*, 168–76.
35. Lartey, *In Living Color*, 67.

from mindsets inculcated by oppressors who treat them as lesser people. Teaching English or learning more about childcare were ways of enabling migrants to become their own agents of change.

Anglo-Australian culture is often applied as a descriptor for Australian culture, even though the cultural makeup of Australia is vastly multiethnic and the White Australia policy was abolished in 1973. This descriptor is true of some other English-speaking nations. Christians are often complicit in such domination due to ethnocentrism. Churches who claim to be multicultural but who do not celebrate the different cultures represented within their horizon of care beyond eating their food at church functions have trivialized the other. This speaks to the need to surrender power if other ethnic groupings are to be liberated. This can seem inconceivable in congregations in which white people hold the power. Caring enough to surrender power for others to flourish comes from the heart of love of God and neighbor. In Phil 2:5–8 we read that Jesus surrendered his power to identify with humankind, and awareness, education, confrontation of oppression, and the pastoral skills of liberating and empowering bring this truth into the arena of the four initiatives.

Advocacy is an important facet of pastoral care,[36] and while individual care by participants was valuable, there was little evidence of systemic or political care. Public policies affect individuals, and this should be considered by pastoral carers.[37] Are church members interculturally educated to advocate for the rights of others and to empower them? Is there a willingness to learn how to surrender power in favor of a common voice and shared power? The services offered by the four congregations provided an opportunity for congregants to be taught, through their reflection on these activities, to become intercultural congregations motivated to advocate for ethnic minorities. Advocating on a personal and national level is a natural extension of pastoral care, for when we love others, we desire their liberation.

Surrendering his power enabled Jesus to love humankind empathically as fellow humans. His death and resurrection from a chosen place of weakness was an empowering event in history. We also empower others by surrendering our power. In the context of empowering migrants, participants had the opportunity to submit their teaching ability to the pastoral calling to listen and understand rather than be heard and understood. They

---

36. Ramsay, *Pastoral Care and Counselling*, 3.
37. Miller-McLemore, "Human Web."

had the opportunity to foster deep connections when the hearts and minds of others opened to the gifts offered by joyfully accepting the gifts offered in return. Accepting the gifts offered by migrants can empower them to love and to assert their common humanity as all parties benefit from the shared riches and wisdom. This person-centered approach challenges traditional and outdated welfare models characterized by a power differentiation between caregiver and care seeker. A hospitality of difference requires understanding between the connections of knowledge and power and the function of power in forming "the other." We need affinity, not identity or solidarity, if we are to be hospitable to the other.[38]

An acknowledgment of the power in others (which at times is unknown or unacknowledged) is a reminder to create space for their self-expression and thus create mutuality in relationships. Creating a sense of mutual empowerment was difficult at Digswell, where volunteers considered themselves as needing to give without appreciating that they also needed to receive. Empowering others by this definition challenges a welfare model that seeks to provide a nonreciprocal model of care for those in need. This would, for instance, be the case at most food banks. A person-centered approach to care enables individuals to assert themselves and have their preferences considered.

Advocacy creates a path to the empowerment of others in any sector or context. Volunteers at each initiative were in a strong position for advocacy based on their own lived experiences and current activities in helping migrants. This affords greater empathy and perhaps influence in petitioning for the needs of migrants for whom the need to learn English, access health care, or train for employment were prioritized by the sponsoring churches. Pastoral support and education were very real, but potential for effective advocacy was unfortunately neither conceived nor realized by any groups.

Prophetic care can have various meanings that resemble the function of "liberating." This involves raising awareness of the forces dominating and oppressing others and requires examining settings critically for the causes of inequality and exploring how we might help change this.[39] Small sparks of this form of prophetic care were emergent at all four locations but not overtly intended or understood as such. It seemed that all functions of pastoral care were apparent but with enormous potential for development. Practices of friendship and hospitality created spaces in which the

---

38. Streufert, "Affinity for Difference."
39. Lartey, *In Living Color*, 67.

functions of pastoral care could operate. The person and life of Jesus provided a model that invited volunteers to offer a friendship that heals and restores new migrants by speaking to spiritual and emotional needs. A sustaining presence became apparent through hospitality and offers of friendship at initiatives, and, in its best form, this would be on the migrants' own terms. Participants helped others identify and activate internal resources, making reconciliation possible by signposting pathways to greater healing of cultural divisions in a safe environment. Embodied listening, prayer with and for migrants, and help with language skills, so important for recently arrived migrants, offered nurture. Advocacy in a context of mutuality offered empowerment to the disenfranchised, including many migrants and refugees, and had the capacity to become a facet of holistic care emerging from church-based, intercultural initiatives. Embryonic prophetic care was in evidence, but theological reflection in the context of reflective practice would have offered further windows of understanding into this vital pastoral dimension.

Throughout this chapter we have noted that, with a few exceptions, the functions of pastoral care were observed randomly at the initiatives, with the exception of Northern Training, where an intentional culture of care was established. This culture was at the forefront of the minds of volunteers at Northern Training, who readily spoke of the culture of care for students and staff. I was told staff who did not buy into this culture were moved along, and this speaks to the importance of selection of volunteers through informal interview processes and regular group reflection. Where this is absent, mature, committed care will be, at best, haphazard.

QUESTIONS FOR REFLECTION AND DISCUSSION

- Which of the functions of pastoral care are operant at your church-based initiative?
- Are any functions missing from which the initiative might benefit?

7

Expressing Love

Sally was marking assignments at the back of the classroom while her students worked individually. "I've spent ages trying to mark this paper," she told me. "I'm determined to read it, but the student is Sri Lankan and has curled all her letters like she would when writing Tamil." Many teachers would have given up, but Sally appreciated the difficulties of writing in a second language and was committed to the success of her students. She chose to persevere with marking the assignment.

PASTORAL CARE AS A discipline addresses love of God and neighbor. Sims notes that the disciplines of pastoral care and practical theology overlap,[1] revealing a pastoral horizon "informed by a determination to encounter and nurture the divine wherever it is found in human individuals and communities."[2] This pastoral horizon embraces local church mission, and Sims highlights these intersecting interests and principles of mission and pastoral care:

> Again and again I have been confronted with how central relationships are to the mission of the Church. Can mission happen otherwise when the God of love in Christ commands that we love our neighbour? My belief now is that pastoral care gives *credibility* to our mission. Without pastoral care, our mission is "a noisy gong or a clanging cymbal" (1 Cor. 13:1).[3]

1. Sims, "Response to Stephen Pattison," 285.
2. Pattison, "Is Pastoral Care Dead?," 8.
3. Sims, "Response to Stephen Pattison," 286 (emphasis original).

Our relationships with God, self, and community render us sensitive to the needs and aspirations of others. Pastoral care becomes an expression of love of God through loving our neighbor. Love is the very essence of our mission, and as we are sensitive to the needs and aspirations of others, we offer pastoral care as an expression of love of God and neighbor. Jesus stated that people will know we are his disciples by our love for one another. Love then, is our most distinguishing feature as Christ-followers. Was this love expressed at the four initiatives? This chapter will explore themes of empathy and compassion, hospitality, spirituality for pastoral care and mission, and balancing corporate identity with individualism and self-care.

The initiatives I studied aimed to address human need through activities, ranging from learning English to assisting integration into society to training childcare workers hopeful of employment. If "pastoral care is an expression of human concern through activities,"[4] essentially expressions of love, then this can include counseling or celebrating or simply being present with people.

For Doehring, pastoral care takes many forms and in North America often takes the form of crisis intervention followed by supportive care. She describes this as spiritual care that comes alongside others to offer sustaining presence in either an ongoing way or through difficult seasons.[5] Developing internal resilience through tough times is where Lartey sees that "pastoral caregivers have a concern for what meets the eye about human persons as well as what may lie deeply buried within them."[6] The pastoral value of sustaining presence often resonated strongly and sometimes by implication with this research into the ministry provided by participants. However, all initiatives provided sustenance by way of multifaceted activities.

Both Bosch and Kirk believe that mission should include, but not be limited to evangelism.[7] Kirk suggests the local church is engaged in mission when it cares for people in the community, and this includes gospel proclamation. The extent to which this emerged in the study and the tensions between gospel proclamation and pastoral care will be explored in the following chapter. Themes of friendship and journeying with others will be considered as implicit suggestions for meaningful relationship building, ministry of presence, and elements of mutuality between volunteers and students.

4. Lartey, *In Living Color*, 25–26.
5. Doehring, *Practice of Pastoral Care*, xxii.
6. Lartey, *In Living Color*, 26.
7. Bosch, *Transforming Mission*, 512–18; Kirk, *What Is Mission?*, 205–25.

Using the combined lenses of mission and pastoral care, discussion of the implicit and explicit theologies of participants will argue that the initiatives offered pastoral care in and through a specific service such as English conversation classes, job training, or practical skills. The three major categories from the data—expressing love, motivations, and skills—will engage Lartey's functions of pastoral care,[8] and his pastoral resources will be used to critically assess how volunteers might have developed and improved the standards of pastoral care observed.[9]

Caregivers addressed in the literature are often specialists, professionals, or interns, so it would be unrealistic to expect the mostly volunteer workers to perform as qualified pastoral carers. However, their effectiveness as intercultural pastoral carers will be assessed simply on their ability to communicate love. The following discussion is guided by the finding that participants were motivated by a desire to see migrants flourish in Australia. All participants, whether practicing Christians or not, acted on behalf of the sponsoring church, prompting a working assumption that they, therefore, possessed some level of concern about the well-being, and perhaps the spiritual well-being, of migrants. The provision of a community service is a form of spiritual care, but given the level of mutuality, this care could also be extended through the formation and maintenance of friendships.

Because of this overlap between pastoral care and mission, in a practical theological framework, each has a spiritual element, and the source of that spiritual element, or love, is God. Mission is at the heart of the church, and when mission and pastoral care are undertaken, evangelism may take place.

EMPATHY AND COMPASSION

According to Lartey, empathy has "three characteristics . . . a *feeling* (affective) level, a *thinking* (cognitive) level and a *tendency to action* (conative) level. Empathy then, is a way of being with other people, which enters into how it feels like to be who they are."[10] While it was not possible to observe and trace the feelings of participants, a cognitive level of empathy was expressed during interviews as participants spoke with understanding of the

---

8. Lartey, *In Living Color*, 60–68.
9. Lartey, *In Living Color*, 68–78.
10. Lartey, *In Living Color*, 92 (emphasis original).

difficulties faced by new migrants and related these to their own experiences. This was then fed back into their volunteering or work.

The intercultural dimensions of empathy and compassion are central in pastoral care. This requires an ability to step into the other person's emotional experience while remaining fully aware of our own emotional reality.[11] Participants at Northern Training demonstrated such empathy through boundaried emotional involvement with students. Volunteers at Swindon spoke of a desire to help their students learn English based on their own experience of living overseas, having to study a foreign language, or observing a family member from overseas adjust to life in Australia.

Empathy requires discipline as we attempt to see the experiences of others from their perspective. This requires both cognitive and emotional engagement to understand the meanings another person attaches to their experiences.[12] Participants were engaged in mission, often through formation in the disciplined exercise of empathic listening. This results in sharing feelings through active imagination rather than projection.[13] For Pembroke, whether in the parish or health care context, care that is "built on a foundation of empathy and compassion is an expression of *agape* . . . a commitment to extend oneself in acting in a loving, kind, and beneficent way towards one's neighbor."[14] This is an essential factor if those attending initiatives are to experience and sensitively express God's love.

Pembroke's deceptively simple but pastorally and vocationally complex principle is a highly desirable criterion for selection, training, and formation of volunteers. One participant had previously had little to do with migrants before volunteering at the English lessons, but she was someone who cared deeply for others and this concern was expressed through her plans to serve and her attentive listening and responses to her students.

Shared experiences of migration enabled empathy with new migrants. Cognitive and conative levels of empathy were apparent in the advocacy framework of one person's provision of medical care for women who rarely received the level of care enjoyed by other Australians. The affective level may have been there, but it was "acting in a loving, kind, and beneficent way" that counted.

11. Doehring, *Practice of Pastoral Care*, 39–40.
12. Clinebell and McKeever, *Basic Types of Pastoral Care*, 70.
13. Augsburger, *Pastoral Counseling*, 27.
14. Pembroke, "Empathic and Compassionate Healthcare," 134.

PART 2

Intercultural pastoral carers need to progress from sympathy (often counterproductive) to empathy and then to interpathy.[15] Augsburger's definition captures the movement that needs to emerge across the sites, through formation and reflective practice if possible. He revisits and extends comment on interpathy by identifying the core dynamic of this shift in affect as

> an intentional cognitive envisioning of another's thoughts and feelings, even though the thoughts rise from another frame of moral reasoning and the feelings spring from another basis of assumptions. . . . I (the culturally different person) take a foreign perspective, base my thoughts on a foreign assumption, and allow myself to feel the resultant feelings and their cognitive and emotive consequences in personality as I inhabit, insofar as I am capable of inhabiting, a foreign context.[16]

Interpathy was the next learning bridge to be crossed when participants described their feelings or experiences. A truly interpathic caregiver may become as close as possible to being "emic." To be emic is to be a cultural insider, while a cultural outsider is classed as "etic."[17] The aim of the missionary, the anthropologist, or in the case of this study, the intercultural carer, is to move towards an emic stance, even though this is ultimately not entirely possible for someone from a different culture. Formation and training in reflective practice can enhance this skill.

Few people would be naturally interpathic. For Westerners, raised with a worldview that often implies that Western culture is superior, this may be a particular pastoral formation challenge. One participant stated that she did not need to understand the cultures of her students, as she was there to teach them English. While she was naturally empathic, embodying interpathy would have enhanced her caring skills.

Compassion can be described as empathy that results in action, or more accurately, care in action.[18] By this definition, compassion was strongly in evidence at all initiatives. Already open to international students because of her intercultural experience, Jean worried about her students because "they had real trouble getting through to others . . . what their needs were." Another responded to the needs of asylum seekers by initiating the English

15. Lartey, *In Living Color*, 93.
16. Augsburger, *Pastoral Counseling*, 29–30.
17 Pike, et al., *Emics and Etics*.
18. Doehring, *Practice of Pastoral Care*, 43.

lessons at Govan. Some volunteers at Digswell were motivated initially by their belief that, as Christians, they needed to serve in the life of the church, which meant that compassion was harder to discern there. Volunteers had a functional approach to their service and spoke of the women they served in a matter-of-fact manner, and at times with some frustration at their lack of responsiveness to Christianity, indicating some knowledge but no empathy.

Empathy is easier to attain when based on shared experiences, although it is possible to learn. The progression from sympathy to empathy to interpathy is often a reflective journey of self-discovery, and if interpathy involves a progression towards becoming emic, then being a cultural insider is a goal to which pastoral practitioners and anyone in mission can aspire. Empathy is harder to access when care is driven by a desire for conversions, a tension each initiative faced without effective resolution.

A FRIENDLY AND WELCOMING ENVIRONMENT

Hospitality is a gateway to mutuality, friendship, and community, and all initiatives held potential for long-lasting friendships and community building. The biblical theme of hospitality among Christians served to identify aspects of hospitality noted at each project (Isa 58:7; Titus 1:8). Jesus links loving your neighbor as yourself with loving God "with all your heart and with all your soul and with all your mind and with all your strength" (Mark 12:30–31). The church demonstrates the kingdom when it cares for others, aligning with Bevans's prophetic dialogue.[19]

The practices of hospitality and friendship building in a community context should be viewed as key elements of a model of pastoral care. Deep and careful theological reflection upon this theme can inform carers as they reassess the levels of care that they are willing or able to provide and reframe the focus of further training.

How do volunteers learn to welcome strangers? Hospitality can be described as a two-way process in which hosts (volunteers) have much to learn from those at the margins and, indeed, become guests of the migrants attending initiatives. Those of us at the center (however we view this) need those at the margins to challenge our perception of reality and our self-positioning. By doing this, our need to change becomes apparent.[20] This suggests, therefore, that pastoral care and all expressions of mission

19. Bevans, "Theologies of Mission."
20. Ross, "Hospitality."

are two-way processes of hospitality that become a meeting point where an exchange of power teaches and empowers and holds the possibility of transformation for the carer. Most participants at all locations sought to express some form of friendship with attending migrants, and a cultural context of friendliness and welcome were significant findings. While for some this friendship was expressed only in the sessions, others sought to foster relationships at other times. These friendships were life-enhancing and nurturing, especially when attendees were marginalized in Australia due to ethnicity, culture, and limited English.

A commitment to friendship and journeying together (to varying degrees dependent on context) is a realistic expectation of Christian practice in similar intercultural, church-based initiatives. The New Testament teaches hospitality to the stranger. The church is both a people set aside from the world and a people tasked with joining God's mission in the world.[21] Friendships between participants and migrants were marked at times by a mutuality that is important for the formation of genuine friendships.

Hosts and guests have different roles. While "guest" and "stranger" are differentiated in the English language, they are the same term in many languages. Therefore, if strangers (and all participants were initially strangers to their students) don't offer the opportunity for their guests to become hosts, they disrespect and may confuse them. It is not easy for us to become strangers, but it is necessary if new relationships are to be forged. This involves respecting different cultural norms and deferring to our new hosts. It is for them, not us, to decide when we become friends. For us to decide this would be aggressive.[22]

Attendees may not experience aggression, but unthinking colonization or lack of awareness of power may well have the same impact. Hosts hold a great deal of power, and an appreciation of this can challenge volunteers to invite their guests not to become a part of their culture, but to step into a space within which a third, new and shared culture can emerge, one where roles may be exchanged. I am reminded of Pembroke's application of the "relational space" within the Trinity to pastoral care practice. Members are unified, yet with space between them that allows for distinctiveness, a liminal movement potentially empowering and certainly defining of identity.[23]

---

21. Jones, *Evangelistic Love of God*, 61.
22. Gittins, *Gifts and Strangers*, 125–26.
23. Pembroke, *Renewing Pastoral Practice*, 26–28.

Glimpses of friendship were present at the initiatives. While a few volunteers limited their involvement to session times, a few others were concerned to care in any way possible. Northern Training trainers clearly wished to empower students in line with the school's rationale and ethos of care, but where on the training and development agenda were processes for developing empathy, interpathy, and reflective listening skills? Where the aim of an initiative is evangelism, love-in-action may demonstrate truth claims, but the tension remains of creating space for strangers in our lives. This will ultimately result in the distinctions between host and guest being nullified through the creation of a new unity.[24]

We are called to invite the stranger to a safe and friendly place where they can reveal themselves and form friendships. Honest receptivity requires us to invite others to enter our world and make themselves known on their terms and, in so doing, become our friends.[25] In order to do this in an intercultural setting, we acknowledge and contain our tendencies towards ethnocentricity and develop listening skills that take us beyond empathy into interpathy.[26] This necessitates education and intentional formation in growing and developing pastoral and spiritual care skills, which are often lacking in mission preparation and missional settings.

The tutors at Swindon were all polite, but chose to be reserved with the students, something quite different to merely setting boundaries. This approach results in volunteers being unwilling to share their true selves, preventing the possibility of honest and open relationships. While reserve is a common Western, middle-class behavior, guests should be welcomed on their terms, not ours, although within reasonable boundaries. This requires flexibility, while staying true to our real selves.

Without this, the guest is unable to relate to the other person authentically. This did not appear to hinder the teaching of English at Swindon, but it did keep most relationships on a superficial basis, which may have inhibited pastoral presence. The complex dance of mature engagement can be described as receptivity and confrontation, which need to be kept in balance. Receptivity without confrontation results in blandness, which was noted in some relationships between tutor and student at Swindon.

---

24. Nouwen, *Reaching Out*, 67.
25. Nouwen, *Reaching Out*, 98.
26. Augsburger, *Pastoral Counseling*, 27–32.

PART 2

Confrontation without receptivity results in destructive aggression—an element of many misguided evangelistic efforts.[27]

This balance is a deep pastoral and personal life skill that can be taught. It could be argued that tutors should not be expected to share personally of themselves, but much depends on the aim of the initiative and professional/contextual protocols. If the aim is to express God's love, then showing one's true self in contextually appropriate ways would be an asset. This is also a culturally bound sensibility, which may require someone from a reserved host culture to be more open with others than they find comfortable.

Learning to be nice is a form of cultural conditioning, so we would expect those with this cultural framework to adapt slowly to a more open manner of relating. Helping volunteers to understand their own cultures and explore their pastoral style could encourage a genuine stance among others.

Trainers at Northern Training saw their students weekly, for a prolonged time. This factor and their strongly held commitment to empowering the women helped them to get to know one another well. They had a down-to-earth manner with the students and managed class discipline when necessary. Students knew what trainers were thinking, while also knowing that they cared, creating an open and honest environment in which deeper levels of relationship were possible. A loving Christian community was apparent at Northern Training where the culture was one of offering care and attention to students and all other staff. The sense of God's immanence, expressed verbally and through prayer, suggested lives lived close to God's heartbeat. This sense of community is likely to have kept the migrants coming to the initiatives.

Transformational pastoral care happens when community is built between guests and hosts,[28] a concept reflected, the data suggested, in Northern Training's very high retention rates. The community formed by the trainers, who made themselves equally available to students, had an impact. Teaching skills at Swindon were quite varied and yet students kept attending, as did a core number of students at Govan. Perhaps the very fact that the tutors were volunteers, with a personal interest in the students, met a felt need for community and relationships with Australians beyond all the professional bureaucrats they usually encountered. Volunteering offers a powerful symbol of compassion and self-giving that can cover notional

27. Nouwen, *Reaching Out*, 99.
28. Clinebell and McKeever, *Basic Types of Pastoral Care*, 25.

professional deficits. Attending classes with people who were not paid but who chose to be there could have softened feelings of loneliness and isolation, at least in part.

Some cultures place far more value on community than Western culture does, to the extent that people from many cultures do not have a strongly formed view of their identity apart from their community. The Sudanese and Ethiopian women at the sewing club were from tribal cultures. Anguish and memories of trauma are experienced by many migrants from such cultures, often taken from their community and forced to function in isolated units in a culture that places less value in community. Further study into the reasons why migrants choose to attend church-based initiatives is required to enable service providers to tailor initiatives more carefully. It is not just a question of what service to provide but what sort of community we want to offer.

When carers value diversity they begin to learn to live in the intersection of the universal, the cultural, and the individual and develop a willingness to celebrate difference, thus enabling the pastoral carer to communicate care and acceptance.[29] Where diversity is valued and where formation includes this element, people are celebrated.

The findings at Swindon affirmed volunteers for seeing students as individuals, a truism for all, even those from communal cultures. One person thought that it was not necessary for her to understand their cultures, which would prevent her from understanding individuals to any great degree. Volunteers at Digswell saw the culture but missed the individual personalities of the sewing club women and omitted celebrating their identity. Was it because of their emphasis on conversion? If so, this was a tragic loss. To celebrate the other requires carers in any role to step out of their own cultural confines, learn about the cultures and the personalities of others, and sometimes intentionally shelve, bracket, park, or otherwise deal with personal agendas.

Discussion of personality is rare in mission texts, although texts that teach anthropology for mission provide tools for understanding foreign cultures. This possibly results from an emphasis on training in anthropology, a biblical theology of mission, and cultural adjustment for missionaries in formation rather than deeper listening and developed pastoral skills. While such a curriculum offers important background, this may do little

---

29. Lartey, *In Living Color*, 32.

to prepare the missionary, including church-based community workers, to love people through interpersonal, pastoral care.

It is significant that virtually all pastoral care formation literature is accompanied by reflective practice skills developed through, for example, Supervised Theological Field Education (STFE),[30] which is generally church- and parish-based, or, alternatively, Clinical Pastoral Education (CPE), in health care and other settings that may include parishes. Wallace notes, "CPE is a process model of adult education that uses the tools of experiential learning theory and practice. . . . The clinical method of learning is a cyclical transformational reflective model defined as action-reflection-corrective action."[31] While this process is often provided for professionals, it can and does embrace volunteers.

If pastoral and spiritual care formation incorporate such agendas, reflective practice skills should become normative for mission formation and church-based volunteers. It is hoped that the language, pastoral skills, and consequences of love will develop and nurture an emphasis within missions literature that enables missionaries (whatever their context of service) to be emotionally sensitive, interpersonally skillful, and aware that their mission can be expressed in terms of pastoral care as defined in this book.

The personal depth in the formation of pastoral care workers bears little correlation to classical missions training where scant attention is paid to intra- and interpersonal skill development. In such a culture, mission workers will be challenged by the quiet work that is normative for pastoral care. This contrasts with evangelism and mission, where telling the story of one's work, and often claiming a level of success, may be normative. Even when workers do not believe that they were successful, the fact that they sacrificed themselves to try is often applauded. Mission workers who choose not to publicize their work might even be viewed as uncommunicative, given they are often encouraged to speak about their work, both to gain funding and to inspire others to service.

Participants expressed genuine warmth and created a relaxed atmosphere through spontaneous smiles, appropriate gentle touch, and laughter—the gift of something simple and normal. Trainers at Northern Training all expressed warmth, enthusiasm, and care through their words and in their focused attention to every student. This was observed as a form of person-centered care, a clear and strong contemporary theme in Western

30. Floding, "What Is Theological Field Education?," 1.
31. Perry Wallace, *Clinical Pastoral Education*, 22–23.

health care practice that may yet have to enter fully into mission-focused practice in intercultural church settings. This fifty-year-old practice places the care receiver at the center of their own care—their needs and desires are acknowledged or advocated for, potential is acknowledged, and they are empowered to be a major contributor in forming their future.[32]

While the communication of warmth is important for showing care, sensitivity around physical expressions of care, especially in intercultural settings where vulnerability is high, is vital. It is important for volunteers to learn about appropriate behavior and protocols of touch and distance for cultures represented at initiatives. When in doubt, it is better to adopt a reserved manner, but, essentially, warmth in relating and person-centered care are basic skills to develop.

In summary, learning deeper approaches to hospitality is a reasonable expectation of volunteers. We are all both hosts and guests in these and similar situations, and awareness of this enables mutuality in relationships. Two essentials for loving are compassion and a commitment to empowerment. At Northern Training, the formation of a deeply caring community created an opportunity through which the love of God could become a visible reminder of the importance of community for mission and for pastoral care. It is important to value diversity and to appreciate that all humankind is like us, like some others, and like no one else.[33] This has a high value in pastoral formation but is not so well embraced in mission formation.

SPIRITUALITY FOR PASTORAL CARE AND MISSION

Nouwen's movements of spirituality explores "reaching out to our innermost self . . . from loneliness to solitude," thus knowing and nurturing oneself; and reaching out "to our fellow human beings . . . from hostility to hospitality," enabling the establishment of a corporate identity between Christians and a sense of mutuality with all others. The third movement, "reaching out to our God . . . from illusion to prayer," acknowledges our lives as they truly are, recognizes God's transcendence, and includes prayer.[34] As most participants were Christian and all implicitly represented their sponsoring church, a Christian spirituality organized around love of God and

---

32. Clark, *Wellness Nursing*.

33. Paraphrase from Kluckhohn and Murray, "Personality in Nature," 35, quoted in Augsburger, *Pastoral Counseling*, 49.

34. Nouwen, *Reaching Out*, 14, 43, 75.

PART 2

love from God in the person of Christ, love of self and love of others, is the context for discussion.

Christian spirituality may not be readily discernible, as observed at Swindon. A rich inner life will express itself in outward manifestations, in a commitment to living a godly life and in care for others. Care for others is, however, also a societal value, and where participants did not easily speak of their faith, it was not clear whether their care for migrants was rooted in the internal and transcendent movements of spirituality. This is a loss, in that mutual encouragement in fostering a spiritual life was absent, and those attending the initiatives could be less likely to appreciate that the care they received was an expression of God's love.

Mission is a necessarily prophetic dialogue in which deep listening to others precedes engaging in prophetic dialogue as mission. Deep listening is a prerequisite for discernment, a mature pastoral skill and a spiritual discipline. Prayer, contemplation, theological reflection, personal and group Bible study, and understanding cultural trends are necessary for mission.[35] This speaks directly to a core theme of this book and applies equally to practices of pastoral care and mission, especially if we add opportunities for pastoral supervision. The value of being a reflective practitioner is strong and clear, whether the person is a volunteer teaching sewing or leading complex international programs. Perhaps a creative reframe would be to see the loving deeds of volunteers as a testimony to Christ, even though words about Christ are absent. The lack of verbalization about faith at Swindon may conceal a form of Christianity that values spiritual formation less than conversion. This will happen in communities where salvation is considered the same thing as justification, reducing some forms of Christianity to little more than nominalism.[36] This is the belief that once we know we are saved, we need do nothing further. To the extent that this was the case at Swindon, the findings note that volunteers were not marrying their faith journey with their care for migrants, further highlighting the importance of volunteers being encouraged to engage with and speak of their formational journeys, even in selection and application processes.

A deep dimension of life occurs through communion as distinct from communication. This takes place when someone is fully present and transparent with the other through togetherness, availability, and faithfulness.

---

35. Bevans and Ross, *Mission on the Road*, 2–15.
36. Willard, "Spiritual Formation," 48–49.

Such presence is, therefore, a grace.[37] Identity is found in the sphere of life between the individual and others,[38] and, therefore, being available is a personal quality foundational to pastoral care and counseling. The liminal places of connection, where authentic relationship requires us to be transparent and natural within faith that is free and offers freedom, are necessary for incarnational mission. This requires being receptive to the other's pain and giving up our freedom in favor of theirs.[39]

A belief that all interactions with others should be motivated by the desire for conversions can seriously challenge such depth in relationship and a healthy spirituality. A spirituality that emphasizes resting in God's presence can be challenging if successful relating is measured in terms of gospel presentation. When the gospel becomes merely a group of concepts, a collective identity, programs to support a good cause, or an individual's pass into heaven, the life is no longer in it.[40] Such depth is not reserved for specialist areas of care or mission. It is part of the day-to-day disciplines of relating and offers natural and excellent formation for any ministry.

Jesus teaches us to love others as we love ourselves (Luke 10:27), often a difficult concept for Christians warned against selfishness or taught that if we lose our lives then we will gain them. Jesus taught that loving others as much as ourselves is the second greatest commandment (Mark 12:30–31), a benchmark that suggests that to love ourselves and practice self-compassion also provides the psychological flexibility and embracing hospitality important for loving others. When our awareness of God is rooted in a sense of God's love for us, we may gain the sensitivity to discern how God would express his love for others through us. This may involve proclamation, but more often (in the contexts explored in this book) it will be by listening, celebrating others, and through acts of service. This message is not new but needs constant reiteration. We must be aware of dualistic thinking in our approach to evangelism and acts of service, which should be motivated by nothing other than compassion as an expression of love.[41]

Uncomplicated compassion is born in a spirituality deeply rooted in experience of God's love, which consequently responds to others through the eyes of Christ, loving them in whatever manner Christ desires. This

37. Marcel, *Mystery of Being*, 120, referred to in Pembroke, *Art of Listening*, 14–27.
38. Buber, *Knowledge of Man*, referred to in Pembroke, *Art of Listening*, 31.
39. Pembroke, *Art of Listening*, 51.
40. Peterson, foreword to *Christianity beyond Belief*, 10.
41. Stott, *Christian Mission*, ch. 1.

PART 2

form of spirituality does not seek converts by artificially creating opportunities for proclamation, but, rather, rests in the moment of connection, discerning God's will for self and others through the immediacy of communion with Christ. This can be described as being constantly aware of God's presence, and, while it is possible to confuse the means for the end, all we do must be an expression of our love of God.[42] For volunteers at church-based, intercultural initiatives, their work is an expression of their love of God (and God's love for them), rather than an end in itself. This understanding will at times naturally result in gospel proclamation through deeds and words.

Reflective theological and spiritual exploration may serve to renew and reframe the service and activities of church attendees, a process that pastors can support and resource. This diversity enables broader acceptance of different ways of being alive to spirit, faith, or God and enables encounters with people who have an interest in spirituality but not in formal religion.

It should not be assumed that an overtly expressed faith signifies that Nouwen's three levels of spirituality have been nurtured. Some church cultures encourage outward expressions of spirituality, such as comments about what God may be teaching oneself. Where gratitude for forgiveness is considered a route to transformation, rates of transformation are, in reality, often quite low.[43] It is possible, therefore, that rather than being an expression of spirituality, frequent mention of an individual's faith journey may mask a drive to be seen as spiritually mature or the highest-achieving church in the area, or perhaps reflects the "thinking big" mentality of some pastors. Individuals may be unaware of this dynamic.

Where love of God is present, spiritual formation is in evidence. "We love because he first loved us" teaches that divine love always precedes a believer's love (1 John 4:19). Our vocation is to respond to God's love by welcoming God's transformation of our lives.[44] This argument reinforces the point that spiritual formation is necessarily rooted in God's love, which precedes any outward manifestations. To the extent that love was extended, all four initiatives were expressions of God's love and rooted in relationship with God, but was this a contemplative, reflective, and theologically informed spirituality?

42. Lawrence, *Practice of the Presence of God*.
43. Willard, "Spiritual Formation," 48.
44. Greenman, "Spiritual Formation," 25.

The reserved manner of many volunteers at Swindon and Govan may have been an indication that they were not completely comfortable or confident in their roles. Perhaps as the tutors journey with their students this reserve will gradually be overcome, but communicating the person behind the polite face is a formational challenge if closer relationships are desired. Reflective practice can enhance this through case study and group reflection, which develop the capacity to articulate previously unknown or unrecognized feelings, insights, and theological wonderings. Where reserve is a particular characteristic of a congregation, pastors might enable a more natural use of a contextualized, aware language of faith through action/reflection and group work. Spirituality that finds expression in both word and deed can enable care receivers to appreciate that care is not just person-centered but God-centered. This awareness of "use of self" is important for the discipline of pastoral supervision and a relational paradigm of pastoral care, where the carer pays attention to thoughts, feelings, and behaviors. This is not navel-gazing, but rather enables the carer to monitor their responses to others, in order to provide a higher quality of care. This process may deepen empathy, increase respect, and help in the creation of a safe space for others.[45]

Knowing whether participants related to others out of their own need was beyond the scope of this study, notwithstanding the fact that a lack of listening skills and self-awareness often correlates with acting out of need, for such a person is often more concerned to be heard than to hear. Motivation for service is never completely pure, and measures for best practice suggested in the final chapter focus on fostering a deeper understanding of self in relation to others.

Simple joy in volunteering was expressed at Swindon and Govan, which is often indicative of a healthy spirituality, and it seemed that organizers had found a good vocational and personal fit for many of the volunteers. The question "What gives life and brings you joy?" can probe the meaning of healthy spirituality and its link with vocation or task. The findings suggested that enjoyment was coded as both motivation and as expressions of love, indicating that enjoyment in working with migrants enabled healthy relating. A person's spirituality cannot ultimately be assessed by another, but a healthy spirituality in which a Christian maintains a deep relationship with God, self, and others will be expressed in loving deeds. Faith did motivate these volunteers, although they did not generally know how to

---

45. Cooper-White, *Shared Wisdom*, 128.

PART 2

express this in vocational or formational terms, another aspect of reflective practice that was absent.

COMMUNAL IDENTITY: BALANCING INDIVIDUALISM AND SELF-CARE

A communal dimension of spirituality is akin to Nouwen's second movement of spirituality, a movement whereby our evolving relationship to self is brought to fruition through our constantly changing relationships with others.[46] Love has communal dimensions that can be forgotten with the contemporary focus of love of the individual. Where enjoyment in being part of a team was indicated, a strong team identity was inherent.

Individualism inhibits spiritual formation, as we cannot reach spiritual maturity or fullness of life in Christ unless we are rooted in community.[47] This suggests that Christian community in which people tend to act as individuals, not meeting or praying together as a ministry team and failing to embody the views of leaders, is unlikely to enhance growth on either a spiritual or a practical level. Migrants from community-based cultures are unlikely to perceive the Christian life as attractive or even comprehensible if they observe that faith is solely related to the individual.

Churches are too often composed of autonomous individuals, and this was reflected in the lack of coordination and teamwork at two initiatives.[48] This absence was surprising, given the prolonged observation and the church environment surrounding the initiatives. Such individualism can become a default stance in congregations with limited cultural appreciation of the interconnectedness of all life, resulting in an emphasis on personal piety at the expense of group prayer, planning, and action/reflection sessions. These activities help to shape group identity. Culturally determined individualism can be detrimental to the health and witness of initiatives attended by migrants for whom a sense of identity is rooted in the group. This includes practices of joint worship, prayer and reflection, teaching, and Bible study. It is a challenge for all these disciplines to be undertaken by teams conducting church-based initiatives, although group prayer is vital for identity and formation.

---

46. Nouwen, *Reaching Out*, 65.
47. Peterson, *Christ Plays*, 226.
48. Stone, *Evangelism after Christendom*, 9–22.

Theological Action Research (TAR), as described by Cameron et al. offers opportunities for team building through biblical reflection based on activities and service. Teams of church members involved in ministry together reflect on a Bible passage while asking how it speaks to their context, experiences, and reflections. This method provides deep insights, with an additional benefit of team building, a great asset for effective ministry.[49]

Individualism has very different outcomes to personal care and self-awareness; therefore, balance is essential. Although group relating is vitally important, care for our inner selves is a priority because we cannot be hospitable to others if we are, ourselves, lonely, as our loneliness prevents us from forming free space.[50] Thus, if our motivations are primarily self-focused, our ability to celebrate others will be hindered. This is arguably another consequence of using others to satisfy our own needs. Needs-awareness and management of boundaries is another key point of connection with pastoral care formation and mission.[51] Attentiveness to God and dying to self enable us to move to a position of concerned focus on what is before us.[52] Service derived from wrong motives indicates that intrapersonal spirituality needs some work if volunteers are to add value to initiatives. Solitude and reflection (as distinct from loneliness) enable hospitality (rather than hostility). Such service may also be indicative of differing levels of self-awareness, which is developed through increased self-understanding in reflective practice mode.

While group action/reflection sessions are important for the development of a healthy corporate spirituality, the capacity to attend to the inner self through individual action/reflection is also important for this. Participants at Northern Training expressed the connection between inner reflection and practice well, relating their spiritual journeys to their work and often referring to the team dynamic during interviews. Regular prayer times and professional development sessions would certainly have built upon this foundation and served as a good model for the other initiatives. This raises the issue of collegial reflection between projects and an exchange of professional development in intercultural ministry resources at a wider, ecumenical church level. What can projects learn from each other?

49. Cameron et al., *Talking about God in Practice*, 61–101.
50. Nouwen, *Reaching Out*, 101.
51. Palmer, *Active Life*, 47.
52. Palmer, *Active Life*, 58–59.

PART 2

DEEPENING RELATIONSHIPS THROUGH PRAYER AND SPIRITUAL FORMATION

Group prayer is formative in building Christ-centered community. Where group prayer was regularly conducted, participants often spoke of their faith journeys. The two inform and inspire each other. This principle was possibly validated in the negative, since, where group prayer was absent, participants hesitated to discuss their relationship with God or even with others. This may be why it was so difficult to observe or discern from interviews a sense of God's presence at these initiatives.

Prayer is a primary source for developing the discernment necessary to know how God would have us relate to others and focus our service. Earlier discussion noted that self-awareness also enables this and is itself developed through prayer and the nurture of intra-spirituality. If team members do not appreciate the experience of community building through prayer, reflective listening, and being present with God, group discernment is diminished, and effectiveness is compromised. At Northern Training, where prayer and community were fostered, trainers would say that students came in as strangers but left as family. One reason for this may be this balanced individual and group spirituality of care.

Did participants offer themselves to be formed by the churches they attended, and did those churches have resources for adequate formation? It is the responsibility of Christians to nurture their faith, while it is the responsibility of church leadership to enable this to happen. Some clues emerged when core church narratives were considered alongside the aims of the initiatives. The narratives discovered at each location fed into each initiative, indicating that participants were formed by church teachings. A critical review of "church as system" would help volunteers understand how a strong tendency to focus on personal pietism plays a significant role in creating a culture of individuality in participant approaches. This was evident, for instance, in Govan's English classes.

An interculturally informed carer will engage in self-discovery and in relationship with God. The fruit of the Spirit listed in Gal 5:22–23 are embodied expressions of a person's relationship with Christ, revealed through loving acts towards others, which speak so eloquently of the gospel: "By this everyone will know that you are my disciples, if you love one another" (John 13:35). Love must be seen in action to be understood.[53] If the fruit of

---

53. Kirk, *What Is Mission?*, 28.

the Spirit in Christian tradition are seen as manifestations of a person's relationship with Christ, then commitment to growth is important if a believer desires to communicate the love of Christ. Motivations for service are the key to understanding this link.

QUESTIONS FOR REFLECTION AND DISCUSSION

- How is empathy and compassion displayed at your initiative? How might you improve this?
- To what extent are you being formed/are you forming others for service at your intercultural initiative? What could you do to build on this?
- Are you being formed and working together as a team, or are you focusing on individual growth? What could you do to form spiritually together?
- If you acted on your answers to the questions above, would you fulfill more of the functions of pastoral care? Which might these be?

8

Motivations for Service

Bronte had matched the needs of others with her skills in teaching English. Several years before I visited Govan Church of Christ, a group of newly arrived asylum seekers had come to the Sunday service, asking for help. They had been temporarily housed by the government, but the accommodation provided was completely empty: no beds, chairs, or cooking equipment. The visitors spoke to a church member who got everyone's attention immediately following the service. He asked if people with surplus goods might be willing to donate them. At the time, Bronte had extended family at home and had no surplus to offer. She still wanted to help and wondered how she might do this. She decided she could offer English language lessons to the asylum seekers, who gratefully accepted. Kitchen-based English lessons morphed over the years into the lessons I observed at the church on Saturdays, involving numerous church members.

AN EMPOWERMENT MODEL FOR PASTORAL CARE

Pastoral care includes therapy, ministry, social action, empowerment, and personal interaction. Each of the four church-based initiatives might be viewed as a social-action model seeking to redress societal imbalances between locally born residents and migrants. The initiatives also aligned with an empowerment model of pastoral care, which recognizes the good within all people and builds on existing strengths and resources.[1]

---

1. Lartey, *In Living Color*, 33.

Behind each initiative lay a desire to empower migrants to live well and work well within society, undergirded by a non-welfare approach that recognizes the strengths in others. Empowerment means helping others discover latent abilities in an environment of mutual learning (as teachers learn and develop too) and offering person-centered care in the best-practice form so familiar in the health care sector.[2] Volunteers engage new learning about themselves through their interactions with migrants in a mutual process of hospitality and insight.

All initiatives intentionally or unintentionally revealed pastoral care in a variety of modes, mostly implicit and not systematically or intentionally created. Instead, it was an outworking of motivation from within a faith framework. Identifying an appropriate, intentional model linked to initial formation and ongoing reflective practice can enable volunteers to be effectively focused on their delivery of service in an intentional pastoral-care mode. Naming their activities as pastoral care would engage paradigms of ministry, patterns of resourcing, and theological principles in an existing, rich reserve of knowledge, education, and formation. Every initiative started in response to a need, although there was no evidence in three of the locations that they had considered what model would best serve the need. In contrast, Northern Training identified and implemented a model of care that attended to practical and vocational needs but with staff who could be used quite readily for care, with a view to referral. Participants at Northern Training had trained in the skills necessary for delivering the model of care most needed. Their willingness to do whatever was necessary to provide the best care was a strong motivational platform for development of pastoral skills, even if this necessitated stepping out of comfort zones or making additional sacrifice of time.

While there is significant crossover between different models of care, and some may not be appropriate for volunteers, nevertheless pastoral care programs through English classes, sewing equipment, and childcare training are well-suited to further development. A basic aspect of the ministry model for pastoral care is that of service,[3] which includes kindnesses done for others, visiting and comforting, and providing social opportunities and material goods.[4] While these activities are within the role of pastors or other church leaders, the aspects listed here might also be offered

---

2. See "Australian Commission on Safety and Quality."
3. Lartey, *In Living Color*, 56.
4. Lartey, *In Living Color*, 56–57.

by volunteers, provided adequate training and supervision is established. Both the therapeutic and the personal interaction models of care require accredited skills and disciplines. Because volunteers are often the most immediate point of contact, it would have been a significant asset for all these initiatives if all volunteers had been trained within a pastoral care course to develop referral skills for care seekers.

SATISFACTION AND VOCATION

Personal and team satisfaction were strong motivators at Swindon and Northern Training. Exercising our vocation and discovering both skills and deficits has a spiritual value because in encountering others we learn more about life as it truly is, about ourselves, and about God.[5] Therefore, volunteering or teaching migrants offers more than just the sense of satisfaction reported by volunteers. This is grace in action, for, as we serve God in serving others, we may discover the reward of satisfaction and confidence in emerging skills. God wills that we discover the joy of life surrendered to his love. It seems possible that this deep satisfaction and knowing takes place even if the process cannot be described with words. An indication of a good fit or gifting is apparent when a participant "lights up" or appears energized when interacting with others or talking about their role with volunteers. All this was revealed among participants but without opportunity or context to express or articulate the joyful story of a vocation unfolding.

It was not clear at Swindon, Govan, or Digswell whether most volunteers had a sense of call or vocation that they could describe or discern, perhaps because the environment did not support this possibility. There was no intentional connection between volunteering, ongoing training, and deep spiritual connection with God that could then become an expression of worship. When a believer's relationship with God leads to awareness of God's presence, they can develop the sensitivity to discern how to keep learning, and how to respond to others. The Digswell sewing club seemed to keep running because it was already there. A new leader emerged when invited by a former pastor but did not flourish in this role and admitted that it was a means by which she could provide legal advice and parenting training. A new helper arrived because she could sew, and another was simply looking for an avenue of service. There was no sense of review, conversation about vocation, or exploration of best fit through discernment. It seems that

5. Kitwood, *What Is Human?*, 65.

the best rationale for the club was as a means by which the gospel could be communicated and with little consideration of the spiritual or vocational development of volunteers. This sole driver essentially created the lowest common denominator, as there was no real alignment with the main interest of volunteers. The leader may have been wiser to establish a free legal advice clinic for the women, a much better fit for the giftings and interest in empowering women, but the church culture did not encourage this.

The sense of excitement that results from a fit between the desire to serve community needs and the sense that God wants us to address the need was inconsistent at three of the initiatives. These factors came together at Northern Training, resulting in a well-run service that energized both students and trainers and reflected spiritual disciplines articulated in a source they had probably never encountered. Paul VI's *Apostolicam Actuositatem* (1965) outlines the role and requirements for lay leadership in the Catholic Church, stressing the need for internal development among lay leaders as "a continual exercise of faith, hope, and charity."[6] As we meditate on the word of God with faith we learn to discern where God, in whom "we live and move and have our being" (Acts 17:28) is working.

It was only at Northern Training that Christian participants used the language of "calling" to describe motivation for their work, even describing it as "a key part of my week, like Sunday worship." The language of "calling" may be problematic for some, and perhaps the language of "fit" is preferable. While affirming that God clearly calls believers to specific roles, at some initiatives it was apparent that service was engaged in without deep thought about vocation on the part of individual, team, or the sponsoring congregation. The high aims of staff at Northern Training revealed a motivation to do whatever was necessary to empower the lives of the local residents and a sense of vocation that was ready to undertake further development through reflective opportunity.

LOVE AS MOTIVATION FOR SERVICE

The motive of love is a characteristic of pastoral care.[7] More than just a combination of theory and practice, it is important to have a developing pastoral theology that helps others while growing in love ourselves.[8] Our

6. Paul VI, *Apostolicam Actuositatem*, sec. 4.
7. Lartey, *In Living Color*, 29–30.
8. Schieb, "Love as a Starting Point."

considerations of practical theology must be rooted in love—seeking to care for those in need.[9] Love was a motivation for service, observed in action and expressed to migrants, in all the locations studied. All love originates in God, and all people are capable of remarkable feats of love, but this truth needs to be held in tension with the teaching of John 13:35 that others will know we are Christians by our love. It should be the community of Christian love that speaks most clearly of God's love, including a willingness to forgive and be forgiven.[10]

This is an earthy, grounded approach to Christian service, which acknowledges and addresses the reality that Christians who are not perfect can still display a Christian distinctive perhaps not seen in other spheres. Motivation for love has its roots in the relationships within the Trinity, where love is expressed between Father, Son, and Holy Spirit, and from which Jesus was sent into the world to love the world. Christians are called to participate in the *missio Dei*, which is loving by its very nature. This is God revealing God's love for the world through Jesus, in ongoing involvement in the world and in the church. God is for all people,[11] and a recognition that God is already at work in people's lives dispenses with the idolatry that it is up to us to bring others into the kingdom. Instead, we should be asking where we fit into God's purposes for others at our point of contact with them.

EVANGELISM AS MOTIVATION

Evangelism is a core church practice, together with worship, hospitality, and economic sharing.[12] While participants at two sites indicated difficulties with the concept of gospel proclamation during the initiatives, at no point did any participants demonstrate anything that conflicted with their evangelical identity, and the statements of belief of each congregation affirmed this. Evangelism is a way of being that offers others the possibility of experiencing God's holiness. This is deeply attractive.

All the initiatives displayed a countercultural way of being in the world, where greed and personal advancement are sought. For example, volunteers and trainers gave their time freely, served people in need, were

9. Streets, "Love."
10. Stone, *Evangelism after Christendom*, 175–222.
11. Bosch, *Transforming Mission*, 10.
12. Stone, *Evangelism after Christendom*.

mostly warm in their welcome, and tended towards being hospitable, an important part of the whole ministry of evangelism. Evangelism is a necessary component of an evangelical faith. It must be practiced through "proclamation, hospitality, invitation, and initiation if the church is to be faithful in its witness."[13]

Evangelism has normally been reduced to an issue of personal salvation, although its roots can be traced to the *shalom* of the Old Testament, which concerned the whole of life.[14] A belief that there is no point in running church-based initiatives unless the gospel is preached demonstrates a reductionist view, possibly an approach that volunteers at Swindon and Govan reacted against. An alternative approach esteems others by recognizing that felt needs may require addressing before others feel loved by God, a model of holistic evangelism that closely aligns with pastoral care and that may lead to a context or environment for proclamation.

We are not to treat others as a goal or way of achieving a goal,[15] because evangelism should take place in a context of genuine care. Findings at Digswell demonstrated difficulties with this approach, however, as the end clearly influenced the means, which was apparent in the way volunteers spoke of the women at the sewing club as "difficult" or "resistant." This approach sets out to proselytize, rather than allowing the subject of faith to be raised by care seekers.

Stone concludes that verbal proclamation needs to take place within a hospitable context.[16] Where pastoral care and mutuality in relationships are evidenced, issues of identity and community will eventually be raised by guests as a topic for discussion. This is the point at which Christians can be free to express what they believe while also listening appreciatively to the beliefs of others, a situation more likely to arise in an intercultural context if sensitivity to other cultures has been demonstrated.

Differing views regarding evangelism and goals for initiatives may create tension between team members. At Govan, aims were not clearly stated and the level of individualism made it unlikely that this would ever become a topic for group consideration. Such ambivalence about aims and goals creates an uncoordinated approach to care, where volunteers do not relate easily or consult in team settings regarding best practice. This confusion

---

13. Stone, *Evangelism after Christendom*, 49.
14. Stone, *Evangelism after Christendom*, 55–110.
15. Thiessen, *Ethics of Evangelism*, 165.
16. Stone, *Evangelism after Christendom*, 262–63.

of aims was unlikely to communicate anything clearly to those attending, other than the willingness to teach English to migrants.

Desire for the production of converts was apparent at Digswell. Although evangelism may be many different things, it is at its core to be truthful, clear, and incarnated, rather than appealing to a logic of production, achievement, or creating.[17] A pastorally informed approach is always preferable to one that is focused on quantifiable "results." A pastoral orientation includes a person-centered approach to care (and proclamation where appropriate) as a better option. There is nothing ambivalent about genuine person-centered care as a starting point. Our actions will be negatively impacted when we are driven to get results. A results orientation inhibits our ability to discern what is really taking place and to adapt our words and actions accordingly.[18] A pastorally informed approach listens to the voice of God and others and enables us to respond with love rather than react in ways other than loving to the stimuli around us. In order to respond rather than react to stimuli, spiritual and theological formation needs fostering in ways that address self-awareness and the ability to identify reflexive moments from our practice, responses, and previously unacknowledged motivations. These moments of reflective practice prompt learning and insight that encourage us to work out the "why" and "how" of our responses and either to problem solve or celebrate moments of deep connection. This offers clearer purpose and balance whenever the tension between the goals of pastoral care and evangelism emerges. Reflective practice changes us when we realize differences between who we think or say we are and what we do.[19] This is equally as true for Christians in their care of others in church-based settings as it is for other carers. When we understand that life is an encounter with God and others that we cannot avoid, we realize that we must be open to the wisdom other people offer us. Our concern for outcomes will then find its correct place in our lives.[20] An experience of just such an encounter might have encouraged the team at Digswell to value-add to an existing, strong pastoral base for ministry by discovering frequent and encouraging points of celebration as they shared life with the women, rather than observing a vague sense of disappointment because no one had become a Christian.

17. Stone, *Evangelism after Christendom*, 29–54.
18. Palmer, *Active Life*, 73–74.
19. Paterson, "Mirror Mirror."
20. Palmer, *Active Life*, 75.

Participants were already serving incarnationally and sacrificially, an ongoing commitment not to be underestimated or discounted because of ambivalence regarding goals. Authentic Christian living was attractive to others at Northern Training, and trainers outside the Christian faith were happy in their work environment. During genuine, long-term friendships, a person's spiritual identity is likely to be discussed, relieving all parties of the need to create artificial opportunities for proclamation that are inevitably ineffective. Effective incarnational ministry is concerned with the question, "What is appropriate at this time?" No evidence of this happening was noted. A commitment to ongoing personal relationships with migrants was needed, a principle generalizable for any Christian desiring to communicate the gospel in an unforced manner in response to an initiative from others. This would allow for those of other faiths or no faith to share what creates meaning for them.

No participants were observed sharing their Christian faith other than at Digswell. Although conversations about faith seemed forced and awkward during sewing sessions, they appeared to be tolerated by attendees, and perhaps they served an educative purpose with an unquantifiable level of value. Some volunteers at Swindon shared a little of their lives with students outside lessons, although it was not indicated whether they ever spoke of faith with students. Opportunities to do this after students graduated from Northern Training were few, although one teacher mentioned that she enjoyed catching up on news of former students.

While it was not appropriate to share the gospel during initiatives, if this was the sum of evangelism in church life, it seemed insufficient. The initiatives all had great value in themselves, as assessed in these chapters. The church will not truly welcome new believers, however, without environments where we journey with non-Christians in ongoing, mutual relationships. This may be a delight, but it can be hard work, and each initiative offered great opportunities for this to happen. We need to understand others as a starting point for evangelism. We need to know what is important to them, their questions, and what they are wanting. This essentially pastoral task resonates with Kluckhohn and Murray's three aspects of humanness directed towards friendship building and deep listening, cultural awareness, and a basic anthropological understanding.[21] The four initiatives offered a service while creating space for listening and friendship

---

21. Kluckhohn and Murray, "Personality in Nature," 35, referred to in Augsburger, Pastoral Counseling, 49.

building but never really managed to effectively integrate aims, education, vocational formation, and reflective practice. These tensions challenge the expectations of churches and suggest the need to reframe missional reporting and evaluation, both for self-assessment and for informing others. Success in pastoral and spiritual care is difficult to determine, while gaining a convert would be viewed as a clear indicator of success.

For the gospel message to be understood requires contextualizing when presented within a different culture.[22] This is also true of pastoral care. Both require a level of anthropological understanding and wisdom perhaps not yet evident in church-based pastors or volunteers, although it is a reasonable expectation given most congregations will be multicultural. An anthropological understanding is an aid for cross-cultural communication, and there are many resources offering guidance in this.[23] Although pastoral communication is always essential to church life, it is rarely taught as a skill, especially for volunteers in intercultural situations facing the additional complexities of cross-cultural communication within a pastoral framework.

An additional layer of complexity in gospel proclamation exists when migrants have limited skills in the language of the host country. It seems wise then for church volunteers to incarnate the gospel through an ongoing commitment to community initiatives, corporate prayer and discernment, and mutual friendships where both parties self-disclose at a pace and depth decided by the migrant rather than the volunteer. Evangelism is a term encompassing a way of being, which at times may include an invitation to respond to God. The role of bringing *shalom* needs to be understood and acted on among team members, an approach that contrasts to a production mentality, which aims for results or outcomes. Life-bringing relationships with others are formed through listening and building friendships, although the complexities of intercultural friendship building necessitate training.

LIVED THEOLOGIES

The words and behaviors of participants influenced and directed the initiatives and reflected the theological beliefs and motivations behind both the desire to serve and the manner of service. Lived theologies are acted out in the way we live out our views, beliefs, and actions. These theologies can be

---

22. Hiebert, *Anthropological Reflections*, 81–92.

23. See for example Omohundro, *Thinking Like an Anthropologist*; Rynkiewich, *Soul, Self, and Society*.

emotionally influenced and may change accordingly. They may appear to make sense in a certain context, but they do not necessarily possess a core logic derived from a system of belief, either formal or personally created.

Participant attitudes about not forcing the gospel message onto people still embraced the belief that others needed at some point to hear the gospel message. Yet participants rejected the idea that this should take place during the English classes. A first step in understanding our lived theologies is to name them. This can be an enlightening process that shapes a biblical and theological understanding of our beliefs and actions, and an understanding of why we hold to lived theologies can create the possibility for healing and a change in thinking. It is essential for pastoral care and mission in any form to understand the lived theologies communicated through language and behavior, given that they will greatly impact church-based initiatives. Engaging in works of service was often only vaguely associated with a dynamic relationship with God or a particular theology.

Another interpretation of this might be that such ministry is a simple indicator of a life joyfully submitted to serving God. In Matt 5:16, followers of Christ are exhorted to let their light shine before others. This is not a suggestion that service should be an imposed obligation; rather, when we live true to our authentic selves, the result of this will be joyful and life-enhancing for ourselves and others. A group spirituality or identity may also communicate to others whether we truly embody the goodness of God; therefore, group work, individual reflection, or insight through supervision have great value in revealing what is often unknown or barely articulated.

When faith and a sense of God's immanence are hardly mentioned, one might wonder how or whether Christian faith is a motivation for ministry. Motivations lie on a continuum between low and high. Low levels of faith-inspired motivations may result in a service that is no different in effect to any secular not-for-profit agency, but lived theologies will influence church-based initiatives in ways that need closer attention. Again, group work, individual reflection, and supervision are all ways of exploring the lived theologies that either enable or inhibit authentic service. Where faith is not mentioned by volunteers, the question of whether an initiative has Christian distinctives needs to be considered, and perhaps Anton Boisen's "living human document" offers a pastoral and formational rationale.[24] Boisen believed the deep spiritual and emotional struggles of a person are to be respected as much as the Christian and Judaic texts on which we

---

24. See Gerkin, "Reclaiming the Living Human Document," 34.

base our faiths. They should be permitted to speak on their own terms and given as much weight as biblical and Judaic scholarship concerning these foundational texts.

All Christians are shaped by their interpretations of lived experiences, as well as their Christian beliefs, whether or not these are articulated. Some experiences are discontinuous or at odds with broad aspects of the Christian tradition, and believers may not be aware of this.[25] Three types of "text" should be considered in reflective practices of care. The first of these is the "text" of faith-based experience, understood through the context in which faith operates. The second is Scripture and Christian tradition, and how these relate to a person's spirituality and identity; and third, the text of context and culture need to be read.[26]

This model attempts to bridge the gaps between theory and practice, an exercise significantly enabled by group and individual supervision and the skill of individual reflective practice. Theological reflection and supervision seek to integrate these texts,[27] an educative support that none of the four churches offered to participants, and, given the pastoral care framework espoused on the ground, this essential process was crucially absent.

CORE NARRATIVES

The relationship between core theological narratives and practical outcomes had a significant influence (both positive and negative). The cultural and relational dynamics of worship indicate that congregations do listen and act on church teaching, a clear signal that narratives need to be discerned and understood within the context of reflective practice. Unhealthy core narratives (such as the overemphasis on individualism apparent at Govan) can be reflected in unhealthy ways, and again, the absence of review and reflection meant a lost opportunity to discern and develop new ways of service.

How did the research identify the impact of core narratives? Core narratives identified at Swindon were possibly limiting in that no one seemed to know what to do with people once welcomed, largely interacting with them at a superficial level. This highlights the importance of pastors forming narratives that address practically integrated theologies of salvation and spiritual growth. While it can be expected that opportunities to learn and

25. Paver, *Theological Reflection*.
26. Paver, *Theological Reflection*, 33–79.
27. Paver, *Theological Reflection*, 34.

grow were presented in such a large church, inviting people into church life, or accompanying them on their own spiritual explorations was not something for which these volunteers were equipped.

The deep ambivalence towards evangelism indicated a personally and individually developed theology at odds with the context, rather than a belief that had been formed through church life, as seen in the comment "I don't believe God should be shoved down people's throats," without suggesting an integrated and practical alternative.

Volunteers delivered a pleasant, faithful service through which migrants were known by name, given a service (learning English), and for some, given the additional offer of care and friendship. This was all positive and is warmly endorsed. There were few opportunities for all to receive care, if needed, or for further relationship with tutors and other church members, in order to learn about God. A core narrative of members being called to invite others to share in Christian community through both spiritual and social engagement would have strengthened this initiative in expressing love of God and neighbor.

Church life and core narratives had perhaps formed "nice" volunteers with privately held beliefs about faith, rather than volunteers with clear formation for mission and care. The senior pastor wanted the initiative to be a gateway for telling people the gospel message, and yet this group was largely ill-equipped for this. Visits from the Cantonese and Mandarin pastors could encourage ease of conversation (as most students were Chinese), and the possibility of further contact through visits, invitations to social events, or even services would be a very natural way to learn by doing and interacting.

A core narrative at Digswell aimed for converts and effectively formed volunteers whose deepest desire was that their students become Christians rather than risk eternal alienation from God. This can limit interest in any form of mutuality or sharing life with the women attending unless it was in service of the aim of gaining converts. It additionally nullified the opportunity of sharing a rich encounter of mutual joy and learning with the women.

At Govan, the difference between the pastor's desires and goals and those of volunteers was significant, echoing and strengthening the difference in emphasis at Swindon between the senior pastor and volunteers. While volunteers at Govan had been deeply formed by a narrative of personal spiritual engagement that should not be imposed on others, the pastor wanted the initiative to be on a clear pathway to the conversion of attendees. It seemed not to matter that people were simply taught English at the initiative. Christians are called to serve others expecting no reward (Matt 10:8), although this does raise the question of how the church might invite others to learn about God or whether new members would only ever join by passive means, such as moving into the area or finding the church online.

Northern Training had some advantages in identifying and expressing core narratives. Hope International had clearly stated goals that aligned with denominational goals and were adhered to by the Registered Training Organization (RTO) management. The hierarchical nature of church structures, together with the management style of leadership at Northern Training, contrasted with the other three locations, allowing for clearly stated goals to trickle down into individual behaviors. While congregational government is a tenet of many denominations, hierarchical structures enable the job to be done, as illustrated here. The professional nature of the RTO was a significant additional factor in the implementation of core narratives, as employees are commonly expected to align with company vision and goals.

Having considered expressions of love and motivations for service, the following chapter will consider the skills necessary for delivering the service offered at initiatives and the interpersonal skills needed for healthy relating with initiative attendees and other team members.

QUESTIONS FOR REFLECTION AND DISCUSSION

- What are your motivations for offering intercultural care?
- Do you find satisfaction in volunteering at your church-based, intercultural initiative?
- Do you desire to see people become Christians through your initiative?
- Reflect on or discuss together whether it would be appropriate to conduct evangelism. Would you use the initiative as an opportunity to invite others to church events?
- To what extent are you willing to nurture relationship with God and with the people attending the initiative, so they might experience

God's love? How can loving Christian relationships be demonstrated as a group of volunteers?

- Identify together some of your core church narratives. To what extent have these influenced what takes place during initiatives?
- Do any of your core church narratives need to change? Why is this?

9

Skills for Pastoral Care and Mission

"What's the first alphabet?" Jason asked his beginner English class. Three students furtively glanced in my direction, looking for help. "See!" Jason exclaimed to me in the silence that followed his question. "They don't even understand that!" His question about the first letter of the alphabet had unfortunately been lost in frantic thought processes regarding whether cuneiform or hieroglyphics were the first written language. At least, that's where my mind went. Jason spoke English as a second language himself, so teaching English to others was a particular challenge. It was an amusing incident, but I admired Jason's willingness to cross not one but two language barriers to teach English to his Mandarin-speaking students.

THE SERVICES DELIVERED AT the four initiatives required specific skills. Trainers at Northern Training were professionally qualified with high levels of skills in subject matter and teaching, and sewing club volunteers were competent to varying degrees in helping those who attended. The following discussion focuses on major findings regarding participant skills, including a discussion of intercultural competence as a skill for pastoral care and mission.

The low self-awareness that limited teaching abilities and empathy for students can again be addressed through supervision, accountable relationships, spiritual direction, and culturally relevant spiritual disciplines. For example, practicing the simple examen of Ignatius of Loyola means coming before God in the middle and at the end of each day to reflect over events and experiences.[1] Similar teaching has been adapted by numerous modern commentators to become a source of guidance, insight, and discernment.[2] While the examen is noted as a skill for building self-awareness, it can also be viewed as a tool for nurturing spirituality.

The migrants came regularly, responding at a human or spiritual level to the care expressed by the participants and to the sense of community created. We are created for community and will sense an incompleteness without belonging to community in some form (Rom 12:5). When migrants miss and grieve over their home communities, the offer of meeting others on a regular basis in a community of welcome is significant. An intentional response to this was a particular trait at Digswell, and this is a skill focusing the efforts of volunteers in pursuit of a common goal. A goal of conversions resulted in intentionality among volunteers, at times even shared in front of students. Volunteers at Digswell had intentionally prepared by learning about the culture of the women who attended, reflecting their high level of education and ability to self-educate in cross-cultural formation.

CULTURAL INTELLIGENCE

This research indicates that high levels of Cultural Intelligence (CQ)[3] are essential to communicate the love of God and neighbor effectively in church-based, intercultural initiatives.[4] In very simple terms, each participant moves from wanting to love people from different cultures to the ability to effectively express God's love to them.[5]

Culture can be defined as ways of living and viewing life, with underlying meanings attached by a particular group of people. This calls for celebration of diversity, not simply acceptance, as we begin to shed our ethnocentricity. This approach does not celebrate diversity for its own sake, but rather as a valuing of humanity as commonly made in God's image. To celebrate others, we need to become informed about their lives on a

1. Ganss, *Spiritual Exercises*, 131.
2. Palmer, *Active Life*. Palmer argues that contemplation should accompany action, by which he means taking a mindful approach to Christian practice.
3 Ang et al., "Cultural Intelligence."
4. Livermore, *Cultural Intelligence*, 45–56.
5. Livermore, *Cultural Intelligence*, 17.

PART 2

cultural and personal level. Most participants were already on the journey, as they also had come from different countries, and, while no additional training or formation was offered, at least they were not like the person "who knows but one culture [and therefore] knows no culture."[6] While this might be something of an overstatement, we can learn, change, and grow when we encounter people from different cultures. We can let these encounters change our identities and our considerations of who belongs.[7] If all learning is situated,[8] international experiences can open up possibilities for learning and appreciating very different cultures and worldviews. The projects studied offered rich opportunity for developing cultural competence and created a context where cultural assumptions presenting as projections, ideals, and illusions could be challenged and tested. Augsburger offers a relevant image:

> Nothing dissolves our assumptions like salt water, particularly crossing a large amount of it and finding oneself in a totally unfamiliar situation. Accelerated learning and unlearning occur as one discovers the immediate need to discard old givens and assimilate new options.[9]

It cannot be assumed, however, that experiences of migration will naturally develop CQ or an ability to celebrate difference, because we don't always learn from experience. We can stay stuck in the same patterns of thinking if we fail to learn from experience, repeating old ways of thinking and acting.[10] This highlights the numerous losses (in personal and spiritual growth, team development, and best practice in teaching and care) when action/reflection is absent. Volunteers are precious people in the life of a church, and it is tempting to permit anyone who is willing to take part. When volunteers are unable or unwilling to learn through experience, the resultant cost must be reviewed and assessed by leaders.

CQ can be learned and can greatly enhance the efficacy of cross-cultural interactions. A possible weakness in the CQ model, however, is that both intrinsic and extrinsic motivations can improve CQ.[11] This might include a desire to get ahead or secure a business deal. So, growth in CQ

6. Augsburger, *Pastoral Counseling*, 18.
7. Lave and Wenger, *Situated Learning*, 36.
8. Lave and Wenger, *Situated Learning*, 33.
9. Augsburger, *Pastoral Counseling*, 24–25.
10. Carroll and Shaw, *Ethical Maturity*, 263.
11. Van Dyne et al., "Four Factor Model," 304.

may not equate to growth in love. Since pastoral care is born out of relationship with God and a genuine concern for others, extrinsic motivations (such as a desire for good publicity or affirmation) do not resonate with the nature of pastoral care. Being motivated by extrinsic factors might in fact qualitatively limit the efficacy of spiritual care (or any form of mission) and challenge Livermore's argument that increased CQ enables us more effectively to demonstrate love to people of different cultures.[12] This does not of itself negate the effectiveness of CQ for these and other, similar church-based initiatives, but the Christian practitioner may well critique any model not formed in dialogue with pastoral theology and complementary mission theory.

Understanding the principles of CQ can enable volunteers to identify areas for growth in their interactions with migrants. Although all four initiatives were in Australia, migrants do not abandon their birth cultures in the name of cultural integration. Migrants will learn about Australian culture, and culturally aware volunteers are in an ideal situation to teach this in mutually rich ways, even as they make cultural adaptations towards the migrants. Embracing others requires a willingness to step into their worlds and use training and action/reflection to see more clearly the characteristics of their culture. There is a simple but rich economy in such interactions, reflecting the giving and receiving of self within the Trinity.[13]

Limited knowledge of a culture makes it difficult to celebrate a person's otherness, and as a result most personal relating will be on the volunteer's terms, rather than on the terms of those attending. Some participants struggled, therefore, to balance listening and speaking. Such lack of self-awareness and cultural competence hinders the development of a mutually enriching relationship, creating a tension between empathy and ethnocentrism. This leaves us trapped in our ethnocentricity, believing in our cultural superiority. At a deep level we feel that our culture is better than that of others. We counter this when we learn to appreciate the good in others' lives.[14] To the extent that we shed tendencies to ethnocentricity, we can embrace and embody the assertion that all people are "like some [others]."[15] This also supports movement towards interpathy. It is natural

12. Livermore, *Cultural Intelligence*, 12.
13. Volf, *Exclusion and Embrace*, 127.
14. Hiebert and Meneses, *Incarnational Ministry*, 76.
15. Kluckhohn and Murray, "Personality in Nature," 35, quoted in Augsburger, *Pastoral Counseling*, 49.

for us to view the world within our own horizons and to feel natural affinity with others like us. If we take this for granted and view our lives and those like us as the obvious way of seeing the world, we absolutize such views. To care effectively across cultures, we need to be aware that others will have different values and will understand, feel, and think differently to us, based on different life experiences.[16]

This differentiation of self may prove challenging for church-based volunteers who have never been immersed in a foreign culture, but most in this study had this experience. Improving our cultural knowledge is an important step in this direction and can also help in overcoming tendencies to ethnocentricity. Western ethnocentricity has historically tainted well-intentioned missionary efforts, a reflection of the still-held belief that all-things Western provides the lens we see through.[17] A basic anthropological understanding of the deep wisdom and functionality of all cultures will help to combat this tendency.

This discussion suggests that CQ may not have a deep enough reach for truly effective intercultural pastoral care or mission. Cultural knowledge is better interpreted when understood within an anthropological framework, as when different gender roles within a culture are understood, as Livermore suggests.[18] However, the reasons behind different cultural customs would be difficult to appreciate without an understanding that different societies are organized according to a logic that maintains the society's integrity. An applied knowledge of this can enhance insights into how decisions are made among a particular people group.

Cultural knowledge was important for understanding the social dynamics of the Digswell migrants. Sudanese and Ethiopian cultures have a tribal mentality that does not allow for the level of individual choice common within Western cultures. In tribal cultures, relationships are central, and people only view themselves as existing as a part of the group.[19] If something happens to an individual, it happens to the whole group, and what takes place in the community, takes place in the individual. There is little separation between individual and community in life or in death.[20]

---

16. Augsburger, *Pastoral Counseling*, 23.
17. Bevans and Schroeder, *Constants in Context*.
18. Livermore, *Cultural Intelligence*, 57–59.
19. Hiebert and Meneses, *Incarnational Ministry*, 104.
20. Gobo, "Corporate Personality," 65–73, referred to in Hiebert and Meneses, *Incarnational Ministry*, 86.

There was no educational or formational support for the development of cultural knowledge and therefore no cultural metacognition at Digswell. Discounting the communal identity of tribal people ignored the reality that in their previous setting they did not need to be aware of more than surface differences. What they held in common profoundly bound them together. Surface differences of individuals distinguished them from each other, creating balance and demonstrating the huge variety among all people.[21]

A deeper understanding of others comes from listening to their stories—both cultural and personal. High motivational CQ urges us to learn about other cultures. Anthropological insights help to interpret what we learn, but without intentional time journeying with friends from other cultures, it is difficult to discern what matters most, and we miss insights into their unique personhood.

Respect is commonly communicated through body language,[22] affirming the importance of enhancing behavioral CQ in the service of intercultural initiatives. High CQ in this domain is demonstrated by the ability to learn and sensitively mimic body language. Thoughtful practitioners have skills in interpreting body language and appreciate that respectful behavior among people of a given culture may be informed by age, gender, and social status. For instance, it is important among Koreans to know whether one is of higher or lower status than the other, as this will dictate the depth of bow and general deference one affords to others. An exercise in metacognition may, however, suggest that Koreans do not expect people of other nationalities to bow to them outside Korea.

CQ and other cultural competencies provide resources for intercultural pastoral care as well as mission, for it enables the communication of love of God and neighbor.[23] Different cultures need celebrating within church-based initiatives to help volunteers overcome ethnocentricity in a mutual process that values our common humanity. Theories of cultural competence lack one of the elements most vital for mission because they are not rooted in love. Livermore adds to the CQ model by including love, indicating that our ability to love across cultures is not within the model.[24] Without at least genuine interest in others, models of cultural competence may be challenged as conflicted by undeclared goals and self-interest.

21. Augsburger, *Pastoral Counseling*, 25.
22. Doehring, *Practice of Pastoral Care*, 56.
23. Moreau, et al., *Effective Intercultural Communication*.
24. Livermore, *Cultural Intelligence*, 17–20.

Discussion of intercultural considerations for pastoral carers and counselors may be based around Kluckhohn and Murray's theory of humanness.[25] People are more alike than they are different, including biologically, psychologically, spiritually, and in group conformity.[26] Regarding "like some others," links between psychological and sociocultural variables is an important area for intercultural research.[27]

There are six relationships between these variables: culture is personality, personality is culture, personality creates culture, personality mediates culture, personality and culture are parallel systems, personality and culture are parts of an organic system.[28] Regarding "like no other [person],"[29] we note the uniqueness of people, who have their own feelings, perceptions, and experiences. No one else will ever be identical in these ways or in their sufferings.[30] These relationships nuance models of cultural competence, reflect the principles of person-centered care within a pastoral care mode, and remind us that individual personalities exist beyond cultural norms and need celebrating as unique individuals. They also provide an additional rationale for training and formation in the skills and knowledge that undergird pastoral and mission practice.

Intercultural pastoral care should complement Kluckhohn and Murray's three domains of humanness. We gain a better understanding of people from other cultures when we understand the ways individual differences, culture, and shared human characteristics influence people.[31] Our research into different cultures does not reduce people to a group of behaviors; instead, we see them as individuals to be celebrated.[32] These approaches to intercultural exchanges in pastoral care contain the potential for significantly more in-depth relating than the CQ model.

A postmodern understanding of culture romanticizes culture less than traditional approaches and seeks to interpret what is observed, not as

---

25. Kluckhohn and Murray, "Personality in Nature," 35, referred to in Augsburger, *Pastoral Counseling*, 49.

26. Augsburger, *Pastoral Counseling*, 55–56.

27. Augsburger, *Pastoral Counseling*, 61.

28. Augsburger, *Pastoral Counseling*, 62.

29. Kluckhohn and Murray, "Personality in Nature," 35, quoted in Augsburger, *Pastoral Counseling*, 49.

30. Augsburger, *Pastoral Counseling*, 49.

31. Lartey, *In Living Color*, 171.

32. Lartey, *In Living Color*, 165–74.

an unchanging truth about a culture, but rather as a group of people constantly evolving.[33] We seek to build relationships with real-life individuals. This is an ethically robust approach to cultural competence, which enables love of God and neighbor to become an important factor in a manner lacking in the cultural competence models noted above.

A starting point for the acquisition of intercultural competence is perhaps found in a respect for difference as a key pastoral skill or stance.[34] The CQ model does not require this, although it would be a valuable component. Both mission and pastoral care require such respect to communicate love to migrants. These factors enabled data analysis to determine that neither respect for alterity nor cultural competence were clearly understood or knowingly expressed at the initiatives.

CYCLE FOR LIBERATIVE PASTORAL PRACTICE: THE PASTORAL CYCLE

The pedagogical cycle for liberative pastoral care is a tool for pastoral practice rather than a defining characteristic.[35] A slightly modified version of Lartey's pedagogical cycle was used to explore my data. Lartey's phases are: concrete experience is used to (i) inform situational analysis, which is then (ii) analyzed through a theological lens, and (iii) theological analysis is then taken back into the initial situation to form the basis of (iv) a response to the situation. Many practical theologians identify this as the pastoral cycle.[36] While the pastoral cycle was not formally engaged at any of the locations, I found that elements were used at different points.

Liberation theologies evolved in the context of ethnic and cultural oppression,[37] and provide a helpful lens for evaluating the four initiatives. Either a tacit or overt recognition of the need for empowerment of ethnic minorities lay behind the English conversation classes, as they responded to the social isolation of migrants who could not communicate in English. Learning to navigate the many aspects of Australian social life empowered students and helped preserve them from the cultural oppression often

---

33. Gittins, *Living Mission Interculturally*, 33.
34. Doehring, *Practice of Pastoral Care*, 1–4.
35. Lartey, *In Living Color*, 131.
36. See Kinast, *What Are They Saying?*
37. Lartey, *In Living Color*, 118.

experienced in ethnic minorities. Forming friendships with Australians also brought a greater sense of agency.

Bevans's praxis model of theology originated in liberation theology and provides a practice of reflective action that can be applied to any activity.[38] The standpoint and reflective procedures of liberation theologies have informed other contextual theologies, notably social analysis, hermeneutical analysis, and praxis orientation.[39] There is general consensus among practical theologians on these origins, including the "see-judge-act" model of Joseph Cardijn's Catholic Action.[40] Whatever the name or the nuance of difference between the models, action/reflection cycles would benefit many missional initiatives, such as those described in this book.[41]

The multi-contextual approach of Theological Action Research (TAR) will be considered here because this reflects a long-held practice in pastoral and spiritual care in church and health care settings that embrace multidisciplinary care. This is a pastoral cycle in four stages with each stage building on the previous one, a framework for reflection that could readily complement and inform activities at each initiative:

- Experience—what is happening?
- Exploration—why is it happening?
- Reflection—how do we evaluate our experience in dialogue with the Bible and Christian tradition?
- Planning—how will we respond?[42]

Reflective practice at the four locations obviously did not follow this cycle and any theologically reflective processes would have been rudimentary at best. The cycle does not always begin at the same place,[43] offering a flexibility that would suit busy volunteers who may even consider it the role of the pastor to evaluate practice in dialogue with the Bible. Accordingly, implementing the pastoral cycle at church-based initiatives may be less about how it is done and more about how to create a culture that motivates volunteers to engage and a leadership that provides appropriate facilitators

38. Bevans, *Models of Contextual Theology*, 72–73.
39. Lartey, *In Living Color*, 116.
40. Ballard and Pritchard, *Practical Theology in Action*, 82.
41. Bevans, *Models of Contextual Theology*, 70–88.
42. Cameron, *Resourcing Mission*, 9.
43. Cameron, *Resourcing Mission*, 12.

or user-friendly theological resource persons. This may be addressed by consideration of the "why" of action/reflection cycles. Love of others requires ongoing critical reflection resulting in improved professional relationships, increased professionalism, increased impact, changed workplace values or culture, and an increased sense of whether the role is a good fit.[44] This last result is a key theme and would identify the strengths of volunteers and offer affirming exploration for growth and development.

Additional benefits include an increased understanding of the influences that have shaped an individual, essentially a natural focus on core theologies. In a group setting, volunteers can become more aware of the cause and effect of their behaviors and how they align with espoused theological positions and associated cultural sensitivity. Volunteers would be empowered by integrating new theory into practice, and hearing stories from others in the group can create a sense of shared understanding and awareness of how these new ways of implementing change can develop a more united, collaborative team.[45] Well-tested processes such as case studies (with appropriate protocols) can provide reflective moments to be explored with the group so that each participant gains a deeper sense of self-understanding. These practices, although challenging, have potential to develop a deep sense of close, effective community through which volunteers learn and grow in more accurate empathy and self-awareness.

Willingness to dialogue with the Bible as part of the reflective cycle would seem a natural response for most volunteers, especially when spirituality is nurtured and when differences are handled carefully. Although this resonates with the dynamics and processes of TAR, it seems a long way from the reality of two teams at least.[46] This model assumes that all team members are Christians, but sensitive engagement with the pastoral cycle could allow non-Christians to opt out of the process or engage with respect while acknowledging their own beliefs, thereby creating a creative and rich opportunity for dialogue. This could be challenging for some church groups, and others may prefer to conduct the pastoral cycle at a leadership level. Ultimately the decision to implement a model like TAR would first have to be accepted by leadership, because such depth of reflection is rare. A two-stage process, of initial mentoring and guidance, to create a

---

44. Schieb, "Love as a Starting Point," 715; Fook and Gardner, *Practising Critical Reflection*, 56.

45. Fook and Gardner, *Practising Critical Reflection*, 130–37.

46. Cameron et al., *Talking about God in Practice*, 61–108.

culture and ethos of reflective practice primarily, and then TAR, would be important.

The final stage of the pastoral cycle formulates new practices based on critical reflection. For example, in the case of English classes at Govan where deficits in teaching and managing classrooms became evident, new practice might be to have a second tutor to observe student capacity to follow the lessons or tutors to encourage students pastorally to share more about their home cultures to bolster a sense of identity. Reflective practice and supervision work together to develop and enhance ministry.

SYSTEMS THINKING

Although systems thinking was not specifically identified at the initiatives, what was noted was its absence as a skill, with potential to consider all aspects of church life as part of an interrelated system. This is a skill with pastoral dimensions that relates to the development of core narratives that take root and are fostered through teaching and actions. This will be the tight focus of the discussion below, rather than systems thinking as part of a family therapeutic intervention or counseling of an individual.

A systemic approach to church life requires us to see the whole. It allows us to see how all things interrelate rather than seeing each activity as a stand-alone unit. This enables us to see patterns within the whole.[47] Such thinking offers a holistic approach to church life in which sermons, prayer meetings, home group discussions, and community initiatives are linked, and thus enables members to contextually understand, process, and apply their learning. When planning teaching topics, pastoral staff would both feed into and draw from the life of church community initiatives. Systems thinking is important for helping professionals to view clients (in this case, congregation members) as functioning within systems. All influences upon a person are considered.[48] Leaders must look at the whole and see how all parts interact and shape each other. Within a congregation, many aspects of church life create a composite effect, whether in the areas of pastoral care, mission, or even administration. Each part relates to the whole.

An appreciation of systems thinking and its relationship to how core narratives emerge in action enables pastors to relate teaching and core theologies to members' service and to reflect on patterns, themes, inconsistencies,

---

47. Jones, *Evangelistic Love of God*, appendix A.
48. Egan and Reese, *Skilled Helper*, 236–58.

and any areas of ambivalence. When congregational teaching is planned around the formational needs of volunteers, teaching topics can begin to resonate with, feed into, and draw from the life of church community initiatives. Even before COVID-19 struck, less and less frequent church attendance became the norm in Western congregations. With COVID rules in place, many church services became remote, with little opportunity for intentional or informal encounters with pastoral staff. Even during normal times, many people do not attend a home group.[49] This makes a systems approach to church life challenging. Jesus made do with what he had when he performed the miracle of the loaves and fishes (John 6:1–14).[50] Now more than ever, this may be a helpful analogy for contemporary church life where time-poor and fragmented individuals and groups must revisit what it means to belong to community, express care as a community, and be in mission as a community.

SUPERVISION

A natural "fit" between task and vocational ability creates satisfaction. Enjoyment of an activity or positive response to a person tends to prompt or even create a desire for excellence, attention to detail, and a relaxed and accepting demeanor. In his book *Hidden Wholeness*, Palmer describes his personal journey of discovering that we thrive when we do what we are best suited to. He encourages us all to find what that is.[51] This personal and very human response has a professional dimension that pastoral supervision can begin to explore. Supervision is an exercise where a practitioner reflects on their interactions with clients and their wider context, together with their supervisor. This joint reflection results in a higher quality of work and improved relationships and enables supervisees continuously to improve their practice. Therefore, at a minimum, supervision should service four factors:

- The learning and development of the supervisee.
- The clients of the supervisee and the quality of service they receive.
- The organization(s) that employ the supervisee and the effectiveness and efficiency of the organization's work.

---

49. See Meyer, "Why Go to Church?"
50. Cameron, *Resourcing Mission*, 53–54.
51. Palmer, *Hidden Wholeness*.

PART 2

- The ongoing learning and development of the profession in which the supervisee, and possibly the supervisor, work.[52]

The principles behind action/reflection cycles underscore the need for supervision for ministry, for such reflection may act as a form of or part of supervision. For best practice, participants required supervision in their relationships with attendees, and teaching skills are certainly a factor that could have benefited from supervision. Participants inevitably experienced conflict, tensions, challenges, and frustration. A duty of care requires pastors or community leaders to be aware of the dynamics of community initiatives, or else appoint a representative with proactive pastoral supervisory skills to enhance accountability. Initiatives with evangelistic aims can be vulnerable to spiritual abuse by offering a service as a platform for proclamation without seeking the consent of attendees. Many participants were confused and ambivalent about the tension between evangelism and pastoral care, and there was no place to reflect on this. Informal supervision is inadequate if pastors rely on volunteers to approach them about concerns rather than proactively offering support through formal supervision, be it group or individual.

Supervision for accountable practice is now considered normative in church-based ministries, sometimes by a skilled pastoral leader or preferably by someone outside the organization. Pastors are accountable to their denominations and congregations for their behavior, professional development, self-care, and supervision. This is at least in part an acknowledgment of the potential for causing harm. Ideally, church members formally involved in public ministry or tasks should in turn be mentored and held accountable in ways appropriate to their roles as representatives of the church engaged in community services. Failing to do this undervalues community members, removes opportunity for personal and spiritual development, and leaves them vulnerable to spiritual, emotional, and even physical abuse.[53] Each initiative had vulnerable people attending in a context of unequal power between participants and attendees. Supervision, therefore, should be a central concern of churches engaged in pastoral care and mission and offers benefits to both caregiver and care seeker, whether through group or individual action/reflection.

52. Hawkins and Shohet, *Supervision in the Helping Professions*, 60.
53. This aligns with recommendation 16.45 of the Royal Commission into Institutional Responses to Child Sexual Abuse. Australian Royal Commission, *Final Report Recommendations*, rec. 16.45.

SPIRITUAL DIRECTION

Spiritual direction may offer some similar benefits to pastoral supervision but has a distinct role of nurturing and fostering sensitivity to the Spirit, one's relationship with God, and self-understanding.[54] Spiritual directors ask pertinent, searching questions in a nonthreatening manner. In the context of spiritual growth and formation this enables the directee to discern what the Spirit is saying. In spiritual direction the director, or spiritual companion, listens both to the client and the Spirit. This requires fostering the kind of conversations that enable both to attend to the voice of Christ through the Spirit.[55]

Palmer describes the Quaker practice of nurturing circles of trust, a model that is relevant to the teams at the four churches.[56] Both spiritual direction and circles of trust offer fruitful opportunity for groups of Christians to regularly meet together to listen to one another as they discern the work of the Holy Spirit in their lives and for their service. These groups do not function as advice-giving forums, but rather as opportunities for members to hear themselves as they reflect aloud to other group members. Such groups may be a new experience for some congregations, but their potential for fostering spiritual health is considerable and may offer a valuable group equivalent of spiritual direction.

PASTORAL CHARACTERISTICS OF INTERPERSONAL RELATING

While this book is not a study of counseling, for Lartey the characteristics of pastoral counseling are closely related to the skills necessary for personal interrelating: listening, empathy, interpathy, respect, non-possessive warmth, genuineness, concreteness, confrontation, confidentiality, and immediacy.[57] These characteristics are normally communicated nonverbally, through tone of voice, physical expressions, gestures, and even comportment. These characteristics were noted across the spread of volunteers. While some participants were skilled in interpersonal relating, others

---

54. "What Is Spiritual Companioning (Direction)?" The WellSpring Centre prefers to use the term "Spiritual Companionship."
55. Smith, *Spiritual Direction*, 40.
56. Palmer, *Hidden Wholeness*, 71–89.
57. Lartey, *In Living Color*, 88.

lacked those skills that could have enhanced their ability to effectively communicate care and interest to migrants. Embodied listening is important for pastoral care, expressed through tone, voice, and facial expression, and the use of space and time.[58] Able listeners revealed these skills in interviews, but they emerged minimally in the English lessons at Swindon and Govan. There was a tendency to be more concerned to give rather than receive from the women who attended the sewing club, even though most spoke reasonable English. Group conversations tended to center around what one volunteer wanted to say. Listening, in a context of acceptance, could transform this initiative by carrying with it an offer of genuine friendship in which the women are in control and a third space is created where both partners can flourish. Friendships have no chance of flourishing where an agenda is imposed by the more powerful party. It would be helpful to emphasize listening as a teaching skill at churches where English (or whatever the national language is) is taught. This skill has the potential to transform the Digswell initiative.

Pastoral listening and storytelling are natural partners. Storytelling is a foundation for pastoral care and an effective way of forming intercultural friendships and looking for ways to connect with God through the challenges of life, big or small. Pastoral care experienced as story builds relationships and has relevance for the whole community.[59] Listening to the stories of others requires deep, culturally aware listening, as well as the ability to relate stories in turn, be they personal, about others, or concerning biblical truths. Communication can then be more comprehensible across cultural and language divides. Results stemming from this activity include the fostering of a sense of belonging and the cocreation of new stories experienced between caregivers and care seekers.

SELF-IN-RELATIONSHIP AND PERSON-CENTERED CARE

Awareness of self-in-relationship and person-centered care is an important contemporary paradigm for pastoral care that needs appreciation and understanding as well as integration and implementation by volunteers. It may be that person-centered care is less likely to occur when gospel preaching is a priority and evangelism is the focus of activity.

---

58. Doehring, *Practice of Pastoral Care*, 53–71.
59. Doehring, *Practice of Pastoral Care*, xiv–xv.

Participants brought "who" they were into the initiatives, a reality that brings who we are now and who we are becoming into the encounter.[60] Some volunteers at Swindon were well practiced, natural, and self-aware as they expressed love to their students, while others lacked the self-awareness to stop talking and simply listen. Individual attention was often given to students at Northern Training. Conversations between trainers and students at Northern Training contrasted with conversations between volunteers and women at the sewing club. These interactions revealed the degree and depth of self-in-relationship of participants. A guide to the positioning of self-in-relationship is found in the concept of person-centered care, where the care provider is guided by the needs and clarified agendas of the care seeker. An appreciation of this framework for relating provides a benchmark by which volunteers can assess their own interactions.

This paradigm involves listening carefully and surrendering our agenda in the context of pastoral care. Can we learn from dialogue with agencies beyond the church? Widely accepted in health care settings and many other organizations, the principle and stance of person-centered care offers respect and space for care seekers to indicate the directions they wish their care to take. At each initiative the pastoral care offered through education, skill development, and language teaching certainly had elements of person-centered care but without intention or awareness. It is important to learn the foundations of best practice from allied disciplines or sectors. The Australian Commission on Safety and Quality in Health Care states that "person-centered care is health care that respects the patient, their family and carers, and responds to the person's preferences, needs and values. Person-centred care offers respect, emotional support, physical comfort, information, communication, continuity and transition of care."[61]

Most of these aspects undergird or guide pastoral care and were in evidence at each project, so it becomes a question of extending and developing skills rather than initiating them. These paradigms are found in hospitals, aged care, and health care in general and, when implemented in church projects, can add significantly to the quality of care.

How a volunteer's faith has shaped their self is linked to pastoral formation within congregations. Ideally, only members who have responded to an intentional process of formation and training within church life

---

60. Lartey, *In Living Color*, 71.

61. Australian Commission on Safety and Quality in Health Care, *Partnering with Consumers*, 5.

should be selected as volunteers at initiatives involving the local community. When viewed through a lens of pastoral care, focused training and preparation for the initiatives would have included what Lartey describes as "attitude formation."[62] This formation path addresses how a person thinks, feels, and behaves and requires self-awareness and an ability and willingness to change and grow. Of course, formation is a lifelong process, so practice-based supervision and formation would also be desirable. Although churches and team leaders are often keen for volunteers to resource programs, automatic selection is problematic. We can be formed through service, but this must be held in tension with current levels of formation. Effective pastoral leadership develops educational and reflective practice opportunities that help leaders and potential volunteers discern readiness for service and ensure that the entire team is enabled to be their best selves with others. Selection and supervision are important criteria.

STORYTELLING AND THE PASTORAL DIMENSIONS OF NARRATIVE THERAPY

Most people speak about their lives in story form, so pastoral carers are encouraged to become good listeners. There is a cathartic value in expressing our deepest and most meaningful stories.[63] Participants certainly listened compassionately, but without a real appreciation of the power of storytelling and the power of listening to help create healthy community. An unwillingness or inability to travel beside migrants emerged at the initiatives and undermined an incarnational model of ministry. The therapeutic value of listening is clearly relevant to pastoral care. In narrative therapy counselors (and pastoral carers) possess lenses and philosophies for interpreting stories, while the care seeker possesses all the knowledge and frameworks for interpretation of meaning. As a result, narrative therapy is a joint venture in which the counselor (or pastoral carer) does not know the direction of the encounter and therefore explores meanings together with the care seeker. This results in questions being asked by both parties.[64]

The pastoral carer also enables the care seeker to tell their story and explore meanings together if desired. It is the care seeker who will build new meanings or reinforce existing meanings as they experience embodied

---

62. Lartey, *In Living Color*, 69.
63. Lartey, *In Living Color*, 72.
64. Neuger, *Counseling Women*, 35.

listening.[65] Caregivers are to be warned, however, against prematurely adding meaning to a story based on the caregiver's personal narrative or theology.[66] The meaning of a story lies within the storyteller alone, and to overlay a story with our personal perspective can be a form of violation. The transition from outsider to group insider whose voice carries weight is an empowering experience that has deep significance in the context of intercultural care.

All the initiatives were contextually ideal for storytelling, as people sewed together, engaged in English classes, or participated in childcare lessons. Most migrants relish the opportunity to talk about their home countries and relationships, cultural activities, and normal daily events. Often the stories of suffering encountered in leaving their birth country need to find a place to be told. By encouraging a culture of storytelling, caregivers value the previous experiences of migrants, which, in turn, affirms them and sustains identity. This can counteract a tendency for people to dismiss the histories of others unless they have witnessed it. The sense of having to start life again and reestablish credibility is common among migrants. Our sense of self is linked to having a story,[67] and we lose a sense of self if we lose a sense of our personal storyline.[68] A stance of embodied listening affirms the self and is also a healthy, relational approach to mission, offering the care seeker the initiative in introducing concepts of ultimate meaning, should they so desire, in a context of love and respect. This narrative approach avoids forcing verbal proclamation on others and is often absent in missions literature. Even missional church literature seems to focus on telling a message in multiple, albeit incarnational ways, rather than listening to and embracing the stories of others. The need for a different style of church that is more accessible to a contemporary congregation and the need for believers to live a lifestyle that contrasts with society is championed. This certainly conveys a message (including a message of love), but with no clear emphasis on the importance of listening to individuals.[69]

It is important to ask good questions in pastoral narrative conversations as a form of active listening that might be applied at initiatives. Listeners are good conversationalists if they rarely change the subject unless

65. Doehring, *Practice of Pastoral Care*, 53–71.
66. Doehring, *Practice of Pastoral Care*, xv.
67. Lartey, *In Living Color*, 72.
68. Gerkin, *Living Human Document*, 211, referred to by Lartey, *In Living Color*, 72.
69. See, for instance, Roxburgh and Boren, *Introducing the Missional Church*.

bringing the other back on topic, and if they recognize that trust and rapport need to develop between all conversation partners before personal questions are asked.[70] When volunteers become story-listeners, they offer cathartic opportunities to others, and this has potential for community building. Where this did not take place, deeper expressions of incarnational ministry were compromised. While volunteers may be invited by storytellers to explore meanings together, storytellers alone hold the full meaning of their stories. Listening to stories is a relational approach to mission, creating mutuality and adding depth to relationships.

CONCLUSION

The values of intercultural pastoral care are important benchmarks for formation, educational training, and reflective practices. Pastoral care offers a more holistic approach to people outside the church than most missions writing by stressing the importance of mutuality, advocacy, and empowerment and by enabling them to guide conversations in the context of person-centered care. In a post-Christendom context, love among Christians and others is an ever-important signpost to the kingdom of God.[71] This is a foundational principle that resonates with the need for the priority of pastoral care as a central paradigm over verbal proclamation, implying that the latter may only be effective because the former has created both space and opportunity.

Pastoral care emphasizes the importance of interpersonal relating skills, a subject not highlighted in missions literature, yet vitally important for effective relationship and community building in an environment of trust. Intercultural competence is often taught in relation to missions and has strong crossover meaning for intercultural pastoral care. Missions training intersects with pastoral care training in this regard and offers dialogical possibilities for education, training, and formation.

QUESTIONS FOR REFLECTION AND DISCUSSION

- How might volunteers at your intercultural initiative implement the pastoral cycle together? When would you do this and how often?

70. Dinkins, *Narrative Pastoral Counseling*, 50–51.
71. Stone, *Evangelism after Christendom*, 171–276.

- Is anyone outside your group of volunteers supervising you (this could include spiritual direction)? Speak with church leaders about how this might be done.
- What characteristics of interpersonal relating do you find most easy? Which is most challenging and how might you grow in this?
- How self-aware are you? Do your interactions during initiatives focus on what you want to say, or do you encourage others to tell their stories?

10

Mission as Pastoral Care at Church-Based, Intercultural Initiatives

A student at Northern Training was experiencing a time of crisis. She was new to the country and had not yet established support networks. That is, except for the staff at Northern Training. She had confided in Lilly, who gave the student her mobile number with the promise she would answer any time during the day or night. Lilly was taken at her word and had, on occasion, received a late-night phone call from the student, requesting prayer, even though student and teacher professed different religions. Lilly was happy to be able to support her student in this way.

THIS BOOK HAS ESTABLISHED principles that will be the basis for the following recommendations for practice. I have established that church-based, intercultural initiatives will most effectively communicate love of God and neighbor through intercultural pastoral care. This finding is generalizable to any church-based initiative, intercultural or monocultural. It is relevant to any situation where Christians desire to communicate love of God and neighbor, including many situations that have traditionally been viewed solely as mission.

Mission planning and practice should always be informed by the foundational elements of pastoral care. This is true of all mission situations, whether local or overseas. Love is the reason for Christian mission.[1] We are, therefore, required to learn to love well to fulfill our calling in the service of others.

Congregational core narratives directly impact the aims and conduct of church-based, intercultural initiatives. Core narratives played out at each initiative, both positively and negatively. An example of a negative outworking of a core narrative is when narratives of personal growth excluded the importance of group formation. This may be generalized to any initiative run by members of a congregation, in whatever context.

Cultural Intelligence (CQ) and other models of cultural competency are helpful and important for anyone relating cross-culturally. However, these models do not fully account for a person's ability to express love across cultures, and intercultural pastoral care practices fill this gap.

Individualism inhibits or prevents successful communication of love of God and neighbor, group cohesion, and the sharing of aims. Two groups I observed seemed little more than a group of individuals engaged simultaneously in the same activity—something akin to parallel play. Aims, motivations, skills, and spirituality were not shared. I have noted that people need to see Christians living in community together as a signpost of the kingdom and as a means of discipleship even before conversion.[2]

Spirituality needs nurturing in individuals and groups for volunteers to better express love of God and neighbor. Volunteers need enabling to speak about their spiritual journeys if evangelism is ever, in any context, to be effective. When groups fail to pray and discern God's voice together and when they don't speak of God with one another, they are unlikely to speak of God, when appropriate, to others.

The activism of evangelicalism can subsume the pursuit of team-based spirituality and pastoral care formation at church-based initiatives. This may have been the case at three of the initiatives in this study. While volunteers faithfully gave their time and efforts, volunteers at Swindon and Govan seemed to believe their volunteering could be effective when limited to initiative sessions, plus, in some cases, lesson preparation. This attitude appeared to be a blind spot, with the importance of spiritually formed group cohesion not considered, or in the case of Swindon, rejected by volunteers who had requested fewer team meetings—bringing the total to only one every five months.

1. "Cape Town Commitment."
2. Stone, introduction to *Evangelism after Christendom*, 9–21.

PART 2

Enjoyment and personal satisfaction may be a stronger motivation than faith for volunteers at church-based initiatives. This was apparent at Swindon where some volunteers stated they viewed their service at the initiative to be a vital part of their week yet were reticent to talk about relationship with God. Personal satisfaction may, however, be an indication of good "fit" where God-given giftings meet service.

Motivations affect the way initiatives are conducted. These should be agreed to during selection procedures and monitored for alignment during group sessions. For instance, attitudes towards gospel proclamation during initiatives should be agreed on by all volunteers.

Framing church-based, intercultural initiatives primarily as vehicles for evangelism confuses and compromises the ability of staff and volunteers to express love. This was noted at Digswell, where the women attending were only celebrated in terms of their responsiveness to conversations about Christ. The goals of evangelism will be achieved as volunteers and staff engage in pastoral care. When the functions of pastoral care are enacted, reconciliation with God is more likely. Creating space in relationships, coupled with empathic deep listening, creates the possibility of others raising questions of faith. This is noncoercive evangelism. The remainder of this chapter will make recommendations regarding the integration of these facts and hypotheses in contexts of practice.

RECOMMENDATIONS FOR PRACTICE

"Is pastoral care dead in a mission-led church?" Stephen Pattison asked this question in response to what he saw as the sidelining of the essential principles of pastoral care, even as he supported the necessity for outward-focused witness to the "divine purpose in the world."[3] Pattison is concerned that pastoral care is often relegated to crisis care, with churches failing to listen deeply to those within and outside of the church. This results in a failure to discern where God is already at work and hinders numerical and discipleship growth. The pastoral approach notices and nurtures all creation and should inform our mission, lest it be reduced to a simplistic form of conversionism and the furthering of our personal ideas. If the pastoral approach is engaged correctly, it becomes a vital component of mission.[4]

---

3. Pattison, "Is Pastoral Care Dead?," 7.
4. Pattison, "Is Pastoral Care Dead?," 8–9.

MISSION AS PASTORAL CARE

This holistic approach to pastoral care reflects the motivations of most volunteers, offers guidance for their interactions with those attending, and addresses the desire to be part of seeing God's purposes in the world fulfilled. Love-in-action eloquently proclaims God's presence and creates the context within which questions of identity can be raised by migrants.

In reframing church-based initiatives as intercultural pastoral care, the concept of mission is still strongly evident. Where love of God is expressed, mission naturally takes place. The youth pastor at Swindon stated that it is disingenuous for Christians not to tell others why they engage in acts of service. While ultimately true, it is important to discern when this is appropriate. Such a conversation is likely to be initiated by the other but only after trusting friendships have been established.

Themes of love and empathy, so central to a study of pastoral care, are equally important for mission. In fact, caring *is* the Christian mission, and the functions of pastoral care comprehensively embody and deliver care. As 1 Cor 13:1–13 declares, without love our works of service (or mission) amount to nothing. In 1 John, love for God is primarily expressed through care of others:

> Let us love one another, for love comes from God. Everyone who loves has been born of God and knows God. Whoever does not love does not know God, because God is love. This is how God showed his love among us: He sent his one and only Son into the world that we might live through him. This is love: not that we loved God but that he loved us and sent his Son as an atoning sacrifice for our sins. Dear friends, since God so loved us, we also ought to love one another. (1 John 4: 7–11)

Spirituality for mission as pastoral care is shaped through formation and ongoing nurture, to enable love for God and others with all that heart, will, mind, and strength can offer. Across the initiatives and especially at Northern Training, the study demonstrated that migrants seek care in an environment where they are loved, nurtured, and celebrated within a pastoral framework.

Many of the following implications and suggestions are suited to pastoral/spiritual care formation and certainly mission formation, but they are also geared in their simplicity for use in sermons, church home groups, and lay training before outreach in any mode begins. The mode is one of pastoral care that encompasses all relevant aspects of missions training for church-based, intercultural initiatives. The points that follow indicate the formational, training, and practical priorities that resource the pastoral care framework suggested for intercultural initiatives, such as the four in this book.

Formation for Expressions of Love

The nurture of spirituality enables the knowledge of God's love to grow in Christians so that love of God and neighbor find expression in service. Amid this service, it is easy for volunteers at evangelical church-based initiatives, and those sponsoring their work, to neglect spiritual nurture. I suggest this happens when works are valued over relationships. The perceived bias towards this warrants further study. There are, however, many ways in which church-based initiatives might reclaim a pastoral basis for spiritual care.

A culture where the spiritual formation of a congregation develops through services, home groups, prayer meetings, outreach, and social events can encourage members to reflect on their personal journey of spiritual formation through different forms of prayer and meditation if the practice of individual and group reflection is also encouraged. In evangelical spirituality people encounter God through the Bible. Through reading and believing the authority of the Bible, discerning, and doing God's will, people gain a meaningful spirituality. This is often expressed in evangelism through speaking to others with the ultimate aim of conversion. While this intentional, impassioned, hard work can sometimes be sacrificial in nature (as noted at Digswell), it can also be legalistic and result in a judgmental attitude.[5]

Whether pieties are sacramental, academic, activist, ascetic, or Eastern with their focus on inner peace, each form suits different personalities, and each has strengths and weaknesses.[6] Explorations of these may reawaken spiritual searching in church members if pastors are willing to explore this with their congregations. This diversity of style of faith and spirituality helps people broaden their acceptance of the many ways of being alive to Spirit, faith, or God and enables encounters with those who describe themselves as spiritual but not religious. The key is fostering diversity that opens doors to inclusive, respectful care.

---

5. Johnson, *Pastoral Spirituality*, 69–70.
6. Johnson, *Pastoral Spirituality*, 70–73.

Nouwen's three movements of spirituality also support effective intercultural pastoral care.[7] If such explorations of spirituality and insights into transcendence are developed as key issues for group consideration, this can nurture the foundational beliefs on which the initiatives were supposed to be based. All team members do not need to be practicing Christians, as was seen with the religious diversity at Northern Training, but team discussions or informal conversation can motivate team members to draw on spiritual resources for their acts of service.

Group work encourages, monitors, and maintains accountability between team members, even where time is at a premium, and brief, focused times of relating after each session could range from debriefing to simple affirmation—whatever emerges as important. Encouraging accountable relationships enhances the self-awareness so important for empathy, care, and listening. The team at Northern Training demonstrated how a healthy group identity communicates love and care to staff and students. They simply needed this to extend into intentional group reflection, perhaps with a trained supervisor as facilitator.

Group prayer, so often part of evangelistic mission, is also vital for the nurture of spirituality and the nurture of love that gives substance to our spirituality as pastoral carers. Is there space for prayer in a weekly half-hour team meeting or for occasional longer meetings devoted to prayer together? Meaningful group prayer emphasizes the importance of drawing on God as the source of all creativity. Prayer is the bedrock of community,[8] and shared explorations in contemplative practices of prayer and meditation offer rich resources for becoming aware of God's presence. We cannot "enter God's presence" because we are already there. What we need is awareness of this.[9]

Being aware of and living according to one's values nurtures a spiritual life that has both inner and outer dimensions. Bringing justice to migrants may be a significant driver for some, while providing practical expressions of nurture may be more significant for others. Both are functions of pastoral care. The simple exercise of shared conversation as volunteers select their six top values from a list can begin to challenge and focus activities, goals, and priorities. Other examples of values are caring for those in need, gospel proclamation, gaining a sense of belonging through volunteering, obedience to God through service, and providing the best service possible.

---

7. Nouwen, *Reaching Out*.
8. Nouwen, *Reaching Out*, 107–15.
9. Rohr, *Everything Belongs*, 29.

Being on this reflective journey themselves may also help volunteers to search out, discern, and appreciate the values that drive migrants, a positive opportunity to enhance a mutual and shared pilgrimage with respect and intercultural/interfaith sensitivity.

Loving team relationships create an attractive community that has appeal to others. Evangelism then happens by way of invitation as others are warmly welcomed into that community, thus enabling a journey towards becoming a Christian disciple.[10]

Expressing Intercultural Hospitality

Gaining an understanding of different worldviews and experiencing a curriculum with an introduction to different domains within other cultures can challenge the ethnocentric tendencies that diminish and even devalue pastoral care in intercultural settings. Love and more accurately empathy are, therefore, prompted and fine-tuned when we become aware of our cultural biases and either revise them or hold them more loosely within a critically reflective frame.

It is unrealistic to expect team members (especially volunteers) to research all the cultures represented at each initiative. However, inviting a "cultural informer" to visit the team for a brief session of cultural learning can address the cultural domains of their birth culture, including manners, worldview, cultural hierarchies, education styles, and gender relations. Self-knowledge grows from reflectively comparing other cultures with those of the volunteers or staff. These learning sessions are best presented in a context of emphasizing the intrinsic worth of all cultures and peoples.[11]

The metacognitive, behavioral, and motivational dimensions of CQ can be taught to church-based teams. The team might even complete the CQ self-assessment inventory as a preparatory learning exercise prior to any activity.[12] The inventory is fashioned to suggest areas in which we might be able to learn the parameters, implications, and practical dimensions of CQ. Yet, CQ on its own is simply not enough.

---

10. Jones, *Evangelistic Love of God*, 137.

11. Hesselgrave, *Communicating Christ*, 104–7. See also Gal 3:28: "There is neither Jew nor Gentile, neither slave nor free, nor is there male and female, for you are all one in Christ Jesus."

12. Livermore, *Cultural Intelligence*, 259–67.

The themes that emerge in this book offer a more practical guide to learning, as they can inform CQ and are applicable in a variety of contexts. For instance, the motivation domain of CQ intersects with the discussion concerning motivations for engaging in ministry. The domain of metacognition might be engaged as team members reflect on the impact of their actions on those attending initiatives, and, finally, the behavioral domain of CQ might be addressed as issues of self-awareness are examined as a team. Once we understand our own culture, we are empowered to step aside from our ethnocentricity to appreciate and respect the cultures of others.

How can an environment where intercultural competence, with clear attention to CQ, be developed and valued? The training of pastors in this area, or lack of it, will potentially impact church-based groups. It is not unusual for pastors to have received no intercultural training, despite the ethnic diversity in Western nations. Preferably, they will gain a basic understanding of cultural anthropology or will learn alongside initiative team members. Pastors need to be aware of their own ethnocentric tendencies, and while it may be unrealistic to expect pastors to have a high CQ already, it is not unrealistic to expect this when teams are exercising intercultural ministry in the churches they lead. My study revealed, through absence, that pastors are strategic in encouraging and enabling the reworking of internal church cultures to represent members of all cultures and, where possible, reflect this into the local community through various initiatives. Intercultural seminary training and required professional development in this topic should be a starting point for pastoral ministry training.

Whether volunteers limit friendships with migrants to session times or extend hospitality at other times too is a matter for individual consideration. If evaluation is done in an appreciative manner, it will acknowledge the commitment already being made. Volunteers able to offer more time might be paired with those who have less discretionary time. The encouragement to create space in relationships in which others can truly be themselves is particularly relevant for volunteers interacting with migrants.[13] Opportunities to explore how guest/host roles become flexible and sensitive to context are critical for pastoral formation. An emphasis on storytelling as a foundation for pastoral care reveals an effective way of forming intercultural friendships both as individuals and as groups. Storytelling as a pastoral skill and intentional ministry stance finds ways of connecting

---

13. Nouwen, *Reaching Out*, 65–77.

with God, others, and all creation amidst trials and suffering. Storytelling as pastoral care deepens relationships and strengthens communities.[14]

Building relationships and community are essential skills for both pastoral carer and evangelist. They undergird guest/host sensitivity and can be fostered during group work. This helps create a sense of belonging. Listening to others and mutually sharing stories can enable the gospel to be explained in a natural, unforced manner, avoiding tendencies to objectify those attending church-based initiatives. Sharing life in this way leads to the cocreation of new stories as an expression of mutuality.

These can be explored at group level, as part of basic anthropological training. For instance, the degrees of formality or self-disclosure appropriate to different levels of intercultural friendships would need to be specifically understood for the demographic of each initiative. Exercises might also include biblical reflections, such as an exploration of "Who is my neighbor?" Many biblical narratives reflect deep cultural challenges about important themes of race, religion, family style, or authority.

Time and risk are necessary for developing mutual friendships across cultures but a commitment to explore these challenges is likely to yield deeper levels of relating. It is only as friendships deepen that issues of identity might be raised by migrants. To the extent that initiative attendees have witnessed incarnational living among team members, they may receive glimpses of the love of God within those friendships. Intercultural friendships are risky, as misunderstanding occurs easily, but the pastoral formational skills and practices below are designed to address such conflicts and even welcome them as opportunities for learning.

The TAR (Theological Action Research) movement encourages theological action/reflection within church-based groups. In dialogue with an aspect of church life, significant event, or ministry experience, Scripture passages are examined to gain biblical insights. There would be a strategic sense of immediacy and in-time learning if this were to accompany the weekly routine of initiatives.[15] Theological reflection looks for points of resonance and relevance for a given situation, and, significantly, groups can be transformed into communities of interpretation in which individuals "test their readings against those of others."[16] Being part of this process can become life-giving for volunteers, along with pastors or any external

---

14. Doehring, *Practice of Pastoral Care*, xiv–xv.
15. Cameron et al., *Talking about God in Practice*.
16. Cameron, *Resourcing Mission*, 13.

MISSION AS PASTORAL CARE

resource-person. Texts should be interpreted appropriately, with the use of commentaries and additional resource-persons as part of the dialogue. This is an exciting and fruitful process where practice meets text through the lived experience of volunteers. Engaging with Bible passages together has an advantage in that the text is able to weather disagreements of interpretation. If we witness honest differences of interpretation, we may respect differences in practice.[17] Considerations of the doctrines of a given tradition are important because theology is a means of character formation and nurtures the faith community. This includes defining faithfulness, which in turn creates group distinctiveness. Theology also places a community in juxtaposition with the local culture and the wider world, as it seeks to communicate the faith.[18]

There is great value in having such community care and doing this hard theological work in outreach groups. Inevitably the ideas and practices of such groups, forged through weekly experience and reflection, can enable them to relate their communal identity to the local cultures. Reflection on ministry in one part of the body can change the whole church. While important, I suggest doctrinal considerations are not undertaken by groups until the other aspects of teamwork suggested in this section are functioning well. While it is certainly true that the primary theological identity of a church determines much of its practice, what is currently taking place is usually what groups will discuss first.[19] The immediacy and relevance of fruitful work in this way brings theology, practice, and reflection together.

Reflecting theologically on the aims and outcomes of initiatives does not preclude the involvement of volunteers who do not share the Christian faith. At Northern Training, leaders had carefully established the Christian values of the training school and all staff were expected to work in partnership with this, whatever their religious viewpoint. Because of the love demonstrated between staff and management and towards students, non-Christian staff seemed delighted to cooperate. This can provide a rich opportunity for deeper dialogue and mutual respect while exercising the pastoral function of reconciling relationships based on caring for and empowering migrant communities with diverse cultural and religious traditions. For this reason, the topic of theological action/reflection cycles is

---

17. Cameron, *Resourcing Mission*, 14.

18. Paraphrased from Graham et al., *Theological Reflection*, 10, quoted in Cameron, *Resourcing Mission*, 15.

19. Cameron, *Resourcing Mission*, 5.

PART 2

located in this section on hospitality. Compassion and empathy are healthy motivators for intercultural ministry, richly enhanced through reflective practice and self-awareness to become caring practices that express a theology of presence.[20] In an intercultural context of care, can compassion and empathy truly generate celebration of others, and to what degree do other motivators challenge or support such celebration?

Drawing on the process of admission to Clinical Pastoral Education (CPE) programs, we can identify the role of an initial interview and careful selection process as one of the foundations of reflective practice. Exploring motivations in an interview may serve to discourage some potential workers if they discover their motivations are extrinsic and potentially not life-enhancing for fellow volunteers or those attending the initiative. Simply being aware of drivers may help volunteers to monitor the ebb and flow of motivation as they discuss these at group level. Discussion can provide a vocabulary for individuals to examine personal motivations and lay a foundation for further private discussions between team leaders and volunteers, an expression of informal but intentional supervision. This formational experience is often absent in a volunteer's vocational journey and was not evidenced at any initiative.

Formation in intra- and interpersonal skill development for pastoral care practitioners, many working in settings well beyond the walls of parish ministry, may bear little resemblance to traditional missions training. Since the intercultural settings for the initiatives demonstrated identifiable levels of pastoral care functions, volunteers would clearly benefit from the elements of the formation and training normative for pastoral care as outlined throughout this book. This would inevitably confront them, in a learning context of action/reflection, with the challenges of determining the relationship between pastoral care and evangelism.

Evangelism

While I did not attempt to discover whether church-based, intercultural initiatives should act as a vehicle for evangelism, differing opinions and beliefs among participants were present. Evangelism may be considered as either verbal proclamation, the mode often addressed by volunteers, or proclamation through intentional deeds, which was the more comfortable path for the majority. The drive for the former approach was identified as

20. Augsburger, *Pastoral Counseling*, 17–47.

a potential inhibitor in unconditionally loving and accepting those who attended. Although group discussion of aims and goals based on the teachings of the tradition of the host church will allow for shared understandings of the aims, an important question remains: Are the aims of each initiative understood, agreed upon, and implemented with clear ownership and understanding?

Apart from one project, few participants were primarily concerned with evangelism. Some found the notion of using the initiatives for this purpose to be offensive and objected to the idea of preaching to a captive audience. This unspoken conflict meant that evangelism lost its place at the table of reflection. What does it mean to create an environment where evangelism is safe, positive, and fruitful? How do volunteers value, respect, and celebrate the beliefs of those who attend? Avoiding these questions, and possible conflict, may be why so many evangelical Christians frame proclamation as caring actions, perhaps coupled with occasional verbal proclamation, or as verbal proclamation alone.

A pastoral care model of mission, with all the formational aspects of this model offered to volunteers, can provide a workable and safe response to these questions and to the dilemma of authentic practice. Verbal proclamations of aspects of faith and belief then become statements of identity in an environment of mutuality and hospitality, usually given in response to promptings from care seekers or as a way of articulating what gives meaning to life within that identity. Success in pastoral care is very difficult to define, while success in evangelism (as opposed to mission in a more general sense) is often defined as gaining converts or having people indicate an interest in relationship with God. Volunteers who assess their service to others through an evangelistic lens might not believe their mission is successful without converts. When considered through a pastoral care lens they might begin to view appropriate and timely expressions of care, prompted by the Holy Spirit, as an expression of faithful service and even as an expression of worship.

The concept of faith declaration by way of statements of identity warrants further exploration. It requires the formation of close, mutual relationships enabling others to self-disclose if desired and in which Christians might be invited to reveal what gives them meaning, purpose, and the source of the love they experience. This form of testimony by invitation, far removed from formulaic and strategic testimony, was possible for volunteers to the extent that mutual relationships were created.

PART 2

Pastoral Care Skills in a Missions Context

Ongoing professional development appropriate to role and task is essential for all team members. If we care about people, we wish the very best for them, so how do churches care for their volunteers? An approach based on respect and intentional care rather than a make-do or fill-the-gap mentality will develop growing volunteers who set new learning goals as individuals and teams. Without ongoing skills development, suboptimum service is being offered. While it is appreciated that volunteers already give freely of their time and skills, it is respectful of both their time and skills to invite them to skill development opportunities designed and structured around the logistics and focus of their service.

Professional development may not even be formal. Even at the four initiatives it would have been simple to share experiences, invite suggestions from other team members, use team teaching to model skills, invite an expert from outside, or arrange a brief seminar—anything to create a culture and expectation of learning and effective enhancement of practice. Should a formal curriculum be possible, the following topics could form part of the design.

The development of interpersonal skills for pastoral care requires both self-awareness and commitment to change. Awareness of our behaviors, styles of communication, and beliefs and prejudices affects our ability to express compassion and empathy. In pastoral care formation the commonly used exercise of role-playing and self-reflection can enable caregivers to understand how their behaviors might affect others.[21] Some aspects of self-awareness, such as learning to recognize personal positive and negative character traits, may be more suited to a supervision context given that trust needs to be established as we identify and address the more challenging and often hidden parts of our personality.

Supervision is vital and becoming increasingly mandated, whether as group experiences or with opportunity for one-on-one sessions. Group supervision addresses the individual's response to and interaction with interpersonal relating, team dynamics, team mission and intent, stakeholder engagement, and the wider systemic context.[22] Deeper consideration of an

---

21. Doehring, *Practice of Pastoral Care*, 53–72. CPE-type resources and field education principles offer sound approaches to this issue.

22. Hawkins and Shohet, *Supervision in the Helping Professions*, 211.

individual's contextual dynamics and associated learning needs will provide themes for individual supervision within a specific framework.

The first option is CPE. This option is by far the most demanding and therefore only possible for a few. CPE has long offered an effective framework for formation and ongoing supervision, not just for professional practitioners, but also for volunteers at church-based, intercultural initiatives. As demonstrated over many years, the resources and expertise behind CPE are not locked away behind the professional doors of health care institutions or reserved only for the ordained. Volunteers are catered for,[23] and this can be extended more strategically to parish teams, a community-based center of mission beyond institutions.

CPE is based in experiential learning and a process model of adult learning. This and the clinical method of education allows students to become more aware of their gifts and strengths and provides opportunities for personal growth. The clinical method entails cycles of action/reflection followed by improved action. Both models encourage personal and pastoral growth, improve competency, and encourage reflection for both pastors and laity. The institution (in this case, the church) provides the opportunity for learning through reflection on interactions. The CPE model includes reflections informed by the spiritual tradition of the student, or, in this case, the volunteer, and emotions are explored in relation to interactions with care seekers.[24] This model requires regular group action/reflection sessions, during which individuals reflect and share on their thoughts and behaviors, listen deeply to other team members, and reflect on case studies and word by word accounts of interactions with care seekers. Reflection in this way would fulfill two goals—more effective practice and group development.

Effective oversight, management, and annual appraisals for anyone in pastoral ministry are now mandated in numerous countries worldwide. For example, the Australian Royal Commission into Institutional Responses to Allegations of Child Abuse recommended professional supervision for all people in religious or pastoral ministry.[25] Supervision should be provided by a trained professional or pastoral supervisor independent from

---

23. "Clinical Pastoral Education." The Uniting Church in Australia's website provides further information about these CPE centers: "Traditionally associated with hospital settings, the Centre offers the same accreditation to people engaged in a range of community-based pastoral care roles, either as an employee or volunteer," "Clinical Pastoral Education."

24. Perry Wallace, *Clinical Pastoral Education*, 22–27.

25. Australian Royal Commission, *Final Report Recommendations*, rec. 16.45.

PART 2

the church at which ministry takes place. All people in ministry (which includes volunteers) are to take regular training.[26] These recommendations should challenge local congregations committed to best practice.

Although these recommendations did not result in legislation, they were not rejected and were considered carefully by major denominations. This heralds a major shift in the way pastoral or ministry activities should be conducted by church-based groups. Supervision and training are no longer optional for either pastors or volunteers, and this research has provided a supporting and reinforcing rationale for the latter cohort. The mode within which the projects were conducted is described in this book as a ministry of pastoral care exercised through education, language training, intentional relationships, and skill development projects. Although implementation will be challenging, these recommendations invite each congregation to consider in advance, and as part of the project design, a reasonable and authentic response that fits each role and task or each group and project. The CPE model adapted for congregational use will suit some contexts as each church embraces a culture of supervision, and perhaps pastors and key leaders will use this model, as many do already. Individual and group supervision contracted or built-in to address similar processes in a less structured way may be more acceptable to many, particularly if their potential for fostering spiritual health is understood. Almost 25 percent of students in four recent cohorts training in professional pastoral supervision in Australia reported "supervision of teams of volunteers" as their goal in undertaking this course.[27]

The Quaker practice of nurturing circles of trust is where people regularly meet together to listen to one another as they discern the work of the Holy Spirit in their lives.[28] These groups do not function as advice-giving forums, but as opportunities for members to hear themselves reflecting aloud to the other group members. If this becomes the tenor and character of supervision groups that underlies content, process, and reflective activity, then churches have a valuable resource in their midst.

Clearly, not all the traditional functions of pastoral care will be operant at any one initiative, but if teams learn their meaning and contextual application, discussion of how they are practiced in their distinctive settings

---

26. Australian Royal Commission, *Final Report Recommendations*, rec. 16.47.

27. Stirling College (University of Divinity) pre-course questionnaires (2014–2018) asking students why they were training to become pastoral supervisors.

28. Palmer, *Hidden Wholeness*, 71–89.

can give meaning and purpose to their vocation. Pastors and others trained in pastoral care will be of benefit in guiding the group as they work out how the functions of pastoral care need to operate differently among different cultures. This requires cultural knowledge and the support of cultural informers co-opted from representative migrant communities to develop examples and case studies for group reflective practice. Peer and personal supervision will extend and lend depth to this learning.

Pastors, Supervision of Ministries of the Congregation, and Systems Thinking

The pastor's awareness of the dynamics within each initiative is critical. It is no longer acceptable to be unaware that the level of supervision and oversight provided in churches is now subject to public scrutiny in many countries. Regular visits by pastors to action/reflection sessions following initiatives could be opportunities for teaching and reflection on practice and for discerning the theological or spiritual implications for the team. Effective group supervision, case studies, and verbatim work will not only speak to the formational needs of volunteers but also model a culture of reflective practice for the whole congregation. The spiritual formation of a congregation is a concern of pastoral staff, so equipping team members to make and nurture connections between their actions and relationships with God, themselves, and others is a primary task.

Theological and ordination training generally focuses on the role of pastors to enable their congregations in their spiritual journeys. Ongoing professional development, including supervision, is important for pastors themselves and any ministry within the community of faith. Should annual appraisals of volunteers ensure that effective supervision and training are available? This may become a significant financial cost to the church. Equally there is cost in not providing supervision, including the loss of quality of service and the absence of vocational development. Care should be taken that supervision and reflective practice for volunteers is not neglected, both for accountability purposes and for the enrichment of community life.

In congregational life a holistic approach in which sermons, prayer meetings, home group discussions, and community initiatives are linked together correlates with systems thinking. How connected with the core life of a church are intercultural projects and volunteers? If pastors and staff have meaningful connections with community initiatives this will both feed into and draw from the life of the church. It is important for those in helping professions to view those they support as functioning within systems, and this has relevance for volunteers. All influences upon a person need considering,[29] and "church as system" is a significant point of learning for all persons in ministry. Those in leadership must view the whole of church life to appreciate the ways in which everything interacts. Within a congregation, the many aspects of church life create a composite effect, whether in the areas of pastoral care, mission, or even administration.

Core church narratives emerge either by design or by chance and these will impact the beliefs and actions of the congregation. "Welcoming in the name of Jesus" through the life of the church was a positive core narrative at one initiative that shaped the outreach of the congregation. The emphasis on personal piety at another actually diminished group spirituality and was detrimental to the initiative. A core narrative of seeking converts at a third community-based initiative resulted in difficulties in celebrating the identity and achievements of the women who attended. These action narratives from the community interface of the church challenge or inform core theological narratives. Where is the place for the ensuing dialogue to happen as core narratives are explored and implications considered?

Recognizing the impact of core narratives on volunteer behavior will encourage pastors to carefully critique and form narratives that impact the formation and behaviors of congregants. I have noted how core narratives both enabled and limited the engagement of volunteers at Swindon and Digswell. The emphasis on individual formation at Govan resulted in a lack of team teaching, while possibly encouraging private prayer for attendees. Big thinking and passionate engagement with faith enabled the brave and effective service offered at Northern Training.

A systemic understanding of church life, as suggested by Jones, would enable a more integrated approach to formation of congregants, including practical application of sermons, home group studies, and repeated encouragements from pastors,[30] as noted at Swindon. This would include formation of knowledge, spirituality, and skills. Pastors may need to seek specific training in this approach and engage administrative support, but this is worth the effort considering the direct impact of congregational narratives on volunteering. Systems thinking is a means by which vision statements come to fruition.

29. Egan and Reese, *Skilled Helper*, 236–58.
30. Jones, *Evangelistic Love of God*, 185–203.

Some aspects of volunteering, including the need for supervision, have been professionalized through government mandates, which recommended supervision in contexts like those of this study. In the Australian context this mandate was made by The Royal Commission into Institutional Responses to Child Sexual Abuse in 2018. The study of Northern Training indicated many advantages of professionalizing expressions of love of God and neighbor, although voluntary church-based initiatives are still the most realistic and even preferred choice for many congregations. We can still learn, however, from professional situations such as Northern Training, which teach us what can be achieved by a group of passionate Christians seeking to respond to whatever local needs they discern. Their commitment to excellence resulted in a professional community-based initiative in which staff were trained, paid, and accountable to a professional body.

Volunteer groups can be encouraged to aim for excellence within time and personal constraints, which may be considerable. This book offers case studies of what can be achieved through a professionalized, church-based initiative, perhaps as a resource for volunteer groups deciding what is desirable or possible in their situation. Pastors should be an active part of this process, encouraging, affirming, and contributing their knowledge of mandated requirements such as supervision. Volunteer initiatives should not be viewed as having less value than professionalized situations, as they offer the opportunity for attendees to experience love not motivated by income, from volunteers who may not be able to train professionally. The recommendations in this chapter offer encouragement for both volunteer and paid workers to enable expressions of love of God and neighbor, which can be tailored to suit each situation and the capacities of volunteers and staff.

Volunteers should not be burdened by professional expectations, nor consider their initiative as of lesser benefit than those of trained professionals. The study of Northern Training, however, indicated a commitment to excellence, the giving of time and individual attention outside of lessons, and a general willingness to do whatever was necessary to offer people a service they needed. This commitment, fueled by passionate expressions of faith, is an inspiration to volunteers and a challenge to those not willing to meet, pray, plan, or reflect together. The recommendations in this chapter, if followed in short, regular post-initiative sessions, can enhance practice and reward volunteers with spiritual growth, deeper relationships with other volunteers and attendees, and offer the undivided attention afforded by supervision.

PART 2

Where congregations are motivated and able to offer a professionalized service to meet a local need, this is to be encouraged and supported by church leaders. Larger congregations, such as Swindon, might be challenged to consider this possibility if an audit of community needs warrants this.

CONCLUSION

From my study of four congregations involved in church-based, intercultural initiatives, I have argued that mission should also be understood as pastoral care. This approach enables expressions of love of God and neighbor.

Interpersonal skills, theological action/reflection, accountability, group spiritual practices, and ongoing skills development are important for volunteers at any church-based initiative. They also apply to anyone engaged in mission if love of God and neighbor are to be expressed effectively.

Volunteers provide a valuable and delightful support for the church but are often underestimated, generally lacking resources, and mostly lacking formation. Even more could have been achieved at each of the initiatives if the participants had been more highly esteemed through the provision of deeper spiritual formation, ongoing pastoral care formation, and appropriate supervision and reflective practice opportunities.

The biblical accounts of the good Samaritan, Jesus and the woman at the well, and Jesus washing the disciples' feet encourage us to take risks. They speak of a willingness to serve strangers, the need for reflection, and the importance of adapting behaviors to other cultures, so they might be understood as love-in-action. To the extent the participants in this study did this, they communicated love of God and neighbor. They may have communicated care successfully at times, despite failing to undergird their practice with knowledge and reflection. The suggestions in this book will enable consistent, successful communication of love of God and neighbor.

QUESTIONS FOR REFLECTION AND DISCUSSION

- What have you learned from this book?
- What aspects of learning will you prioritize in your practice of intercultural care?

Bibliography

Paull, Sue, et al. *Responding to CALD Learners: Cultural Diversity in Action.* https://www.education.vic.gov.au/Documents/about/research/acfepublications/caldlearners.pdf.
Ackerman, Phillip L. "A Theory of Adult Intellectual Development: Process, Personality, Interests, and Knowledge." *Intelligence* 22.2 (1996) 227–57.
Ang, Soon, and Linn Van Dyne. "Conceptualizations of Cultural Intelligence: Definition, Distinctiveness, and Nomological Network." In *Handbook of Cultural Intelligence: Theory, Measurement, and Applications,* edited by Soon Ang and Linn Van Dyne, 3–16. London: Routledge, 2015.
Ang, Soon, et al. "Cultural Intelligence: Its Measurement and Effects on Cultural Judgement and Decision Making, Cultural Adaptation and Task Performance." *Management and Organization Review* 3.3 (2007) 335–71.
Arbuckle, Gerald A. *Earthing the Gospel: An Inculturation Handbook for Pastoral Workers.* Homebush, NSW: Society of St Paul, 1990.
Augsburger, David W. *Pastoral Counseling across Cultures.* Philadelphia: Westminster, 1986.
Australian Commission on Safety and Quality in Health Care. *Partnering with Consumers: A Guide for Consumers.* 2023. https://www.safetyandquality.gov.au/sites/default/files/2022-10/partnering_with_consumers_a_guide_for_consumers_-_web_accessible.pdf.
Australian Royal Commission into Institutional Responses to Child Sexual Abuse. *Final Report Recommendations.* 2017. https://www.childabuseroyalcommission.gov.au/sites/default/files/final_report_-_recommendations.pdf.
Ballard, Paul, and John Pritchard. *Practical Theology in Action.* London: SPCK, 1996.
Benner, David G. *Desiring God's Will: Aligning Our Hearts with the Heart of God.* Downers Grove, IL: IVP, 2005.
Bevans, Stephen B. *Models of Contextual Theology.* Maryknoll, NY: Orbis, 2002.
———. "Theologies of Mission." In *The Oxford Handbook of Mission Studies,* edited by Kirsteen Kim and Alison Fitchett-Climenhaga, 111–28. Online ed. Oxford: Oxford Academic, 2022. https://doi.org/10.1093/oxfordhb/9780198831723.001.0001.
Bevans, Stephen B., and Cathy Ross. "Mission as Prophetic Dialogue." In *Mission on the Road to Emmaus: Constants, Context and Prophetic Dialogue,* edited by Cathy Ross and Stephen B. Bevans, 2–15. London: SCM, 2015.
Bevans, Stephen B., and Roger P. Schroeder. *Constants in Context.* Maryknoll, NY: Orbis, 2004.

BIBLIOGRAPHY

Boisen, Anton. *Explorations of the Inner World: A Study of Mental Disorder and Religious Experience*. New York: Willet, Clark & Co., 1936.

Bosch, David J. *Transforming Mission: Paradigm Shifts in Theology of Mission*. Maryknoll, NY: Orbis, 1991.

Bryant, Antony, and Kathy Charmaz. "Grounded Theory Research: Methods and Practices." In *The SAGE Handbook of Grounded Theory*, edited by Antony Bryant and Kathy Charmaz, 1–28. Thousand Oaks, CA: SAGE, 2007.

Buber, Martin. *The Knowledge of Man*. Translated by Maurice Friedman and Ronald Gregor Smith. London: Allen & Unwin, 1965.

Cameron, Helen. *Resourcing Mission: Practical Theology for Changing Churches*. London: SCM, 2010.

Cameron, Helen, et al. *Talking about God in Practice: Theological Action Research and Practical Theology*. London: SCM, 2010.

The Cape Town Commitment: A Confession of Faith and a Call to Action. 2011. The Lausanne Movement. https://www.lausanne.org/content/ctcommitment.

Carroll, Michael, and Elisabeth Shaw. *Ethical Maturity in the Helping Professions: Making Difficult Life and Work Decisions*. London: Jessica Kingsley, 2013.

Ceci, Stephen J. *On Intelligence: A Bioecological Treatise on Intellectual Development*. Expanded ed. Cambridge, MA: Harvard University Press, 1996.

Charmaz, Kathy. *Constructing Grounded Theory: Introducing Qualitative Methods*. 2nd ed. London: SAGE, 2014.

Clark, Carolyn. *Wellness Nursing: Concepts, Theory, Research, and Practice*. New York: Springer, 1986.

Clebsch, William A., and Charles R. Jaekle. *Pastoral Care in Historical Perspective*. Englewood Cliffs, NJ: Prentice-Hall, 1964.

Clifton, Shane. *Pentecostal Churches in Transition: Analysing the Developing Ecclesiology of the Assemblies of God in Australia*. Boston: Brill, 2009.

Clinebell, Howard, and Bridget C. McKeever. *Basic Types of Pastoral Care and Counselling: Resources for the Ministry of Healing and Growth*. London: SCM, 2011.

"Clinical Pastoral Education." Uniting Church in Australia. https://victas.uca.org.au/community-learning/clinical-pastoral-education/.

Colley, Bartholomew Bioh. "A Community Approach to Overcoming Violence: Peace and Justice through Reconciliation." *Ecumenical Review* 53.3 (2001) 385–89.

Cooper-White, Pamela. *Shared Wisdom: Use of Self in Pastoral Care and Counselling*. Minneapolis: Augsburg Fortress, 2001.

Corbin, Juliet, and Anselm Strauss. *Basics of Qualitative Research: Techniques and Procedures for Developing Grounded Theory*. 3rd ed. Thousand Oaks, CA: SAGE, 2008.

Dinkins, Burrell David. *Narrative Pastoral Counseling*. Maitland, FL: Xulon, 2005.

Doehring, Carrie. *The Practice of Pastoral Care: An Intercultural Approach*. Louisville, KY: Westminster John Knox, 2015.

Earley, Christopher, et al. *CQ: Developing Cultural Intelligence at Work*. Stanford: Stanford University Press, 2006.

Evans, Craig A. *Luke*. New International Biblical Commentary: New Testament Series. Peabody, MA: Hendrickson, 1990.

Brotherhood of St Laurence. "Opening Doors: Celebrating the Work of the Ecumenical Migration Centre 1956–2016." 2016. https://library.bsl.org.au/bsljspui/bitstream/1/9341/1/BSL_Opening_doors_celebrating_EMC_2016.pdf.

BIBLIOGRAPHY

Egan, Gerard, and Robert J. Reese. *The Skilled Helper: A Problem-Management and Opportunity-Development Approach to Helping.* 10th ed. Belmont, CA: Brooks/Cole, 2014.

Engel, Rafael J., and Russell K. Schutt. *The Practice of Research in Social Work.* 3rd ed. Thousand Oaks, CA: SAGE, 2013.

Federation of Ethnic Communities' Council of Australia. *Cultural Competence in Australia: A Guide.* 2019. http://fecca.org.au/wp-content/uploads/2019/05/Cultural-Competence-in-Australia-A-Guide.pdf.

Flett, John G. *The Witness of God: The Trinity, Missio Dei, Karl Barth, and the Nature of Christian Community.* Grand Rapids: Eerdmans, 2010.

Flick, Uwe. *Doing Grounded Theory.* London: SAGE, 2018. https://dx.doi.org/10.4135/9781529716658.

Floding, Matthew. "What Is Theological Field Education?" In *Welcome to Theological Field Education*, edited by Matthew Floding, 1–16. Herndon, VA: Rowman & Littlefield, 2011.

Fook, Jan, and Fiona Gardner. *Practising Critical Reflection: A Resource Handbook.* Maidenhead, UK: Open University Press, 2007.

Francis. *Evangelii Gaudium.* Nov. 24, 2013. https://www.vatican.va/content/francesco/en/apost_exhortations/documents/papa-francesco_esortazione-ap_20131124_evangelii-gaudium.html.

Frost, Michael. *Exiles: Living Missionally in a Post-Christian Culture.* Grand Rapids: Baker, 2006.

Frost, Michael, and Alan Hirsch. *The Shaping of Things to Come: Innovation and Mission for the 21st-Century Church.* Grand Rapids: Baker, 2003.

Ganss, George E. *A Translation and Commentary: The Spiritual Exercises of Saint Ignatius.* St. Louis, MO: Institute of Jesuit Sources, 1992.

Geertz, Clifford. *The Interpretation of Cultures.* New York: Basic Books, 1973.

Gerkin, Charles. *The Living Human Document: Revisioning Pastoral Counseling in a Hermeneutical Mode.* Nashville: Abingdon, 1984.

Gerkin, Charles. "Reclaiming the Living Human Document." In *Images of Pastoral Care: Classic Readings*, edited by Robert Dykstra, 30–39. St. Louis, MO: Chalice, 2005.

Gittins, Anthony J. *Gifts and Strangers: Meeting the Challenge of Inculturation.* Mahwah, NJ: Paulist, 1989.

Gittins, Anthony J. *Living Mission Interculturally: Faith, Culture, and the Renewal of Praxis.* Collegeville, MN: Liturgical, 2015.

Glaser, Barney G., and Anselm L. Strauss. *The Discovery of Grounded Theory.* New Brunswick, NJ: Aldine Transaction, 1999.

Gobo, Boganjalo. "Corporate Personality: Ancient Israel and Africa." In *The Challenge of Black Theology in South Africa*, edited by B. Moore. London: C. Hurst, 1973; Atlanta: John Knox Press, 1974.

Graham, Elaine, et al. *Theological Reflection: Methods.* London: SCM, 2005.

Grayston, Kenneth. *The Gospel of John.* Epworth Commentaries. London: Epworth, 1990.

Greenman, Jeffrey P. "Spiritual Formation in Theological Perspective: Classic Issues, Contemporary Challenges." In *Life in the Spirit: Theological Formation in Theological Perspective*, edited by Jeffrey P. Greenman and George Kalantzis, 23–35. Downers Grove, IL: IVP Academic, 2010.

Hall, Edward Twitchell. *The Silent Language.* New York: Doubleday, 1990.

BIBLIOGRAPHY

Hawkins, Peter, and Robin Shohet. *Supervision in the Helping Professions*. 4th ed. Maidenhead, UK: Open University Press, 2012.

Headland, Thomas N., et al., eds. *Emics and Etics: The Insider/Outsider Debate*. Frontiers of Anthropology 7. London: SAGE, 1990.

Henriques-Gomes, Luke. "South Sudanese-Australians Report Racial Abuse Intensified after 'African Gangs' Claims." *Guardian Australia*, Nov. 3, 2018. https://www.theguardian.com/world/2018/nov/04/south-sudanese-australians-report-abuse-intensified-after-african-gangs-claims.

Hesselgrave, David J. *Communicating Christ Cross-Culturally: An Introduction to Missionary Communication*. 2nd ed. Grand Rapids: Zondervan, 1991.

Hiebert, Paul G. *Anthropological Reflections on Missiological Issues*. Grand Rapids: Baker, 1994.

Hiebert, Paul G., and Eloise Hiebert Meneses. *Incarnational Ministry: Planting Churches in Band, Tribal, Peasant, and Urban Societies*. Grand Rapids: Baker, 1995.

Holton, Judith A., and Isabelle Walsh. *Classic Grounded Theory: Applications with Qualitative and Quantitative Data*. Thousand Oaks, CA: SAGE, 2020. https://dx.doi.org/10.4135/9781071802762.

Johnson, Ben Campbell. *Pastoral Spirituality: A Focus for Ministry*. Philadelphia: Westminster, 1988.

Johnson, Timothy Luke. *The Gospel of Luke*. Sacra Pagina 3. Collegeville, MN: Liturgical Press, 2018.

Jones, Scott J. *The Evangelistic Love of God and Neighbor: A Theology of Witness and Discipleship*. Nashville: Abingdon, 2003.

Kennedy, Brianna L., and Robert Thornberg. "Deduction, Induction, and Abduction." In *The SAGE Handbook of Qualitative Data Collection*, edited by Uwe Flick, 49–64. London: SAGE, 2018. https://dx.doi.org/10.4135/9781526416070.n4.

Kim, Kirsteen, and Alison Fitchett-Climenhaga. "Introduction to Mission Studies: Analyzing Missiology's Current Configuration and Charting Future Prospects." In *The Oxford Handbook of Mission Studies*, edited by Kirsteen Kim and Alison Fitchett-Climenhaga, 3–18. Oxford: Oxford Academic, 2022. https://doi-org.divinity.idm.oclc.org/10.1093/oxfordhb/9780198831723.013.43.

Kinast, Robert L. *What Are They Saying about Theological Reflection?* New York: Paulist, 2000.

Kirk, J. Andrew. *What Is Mission? Theological Explorations*. London: Darton, Longman & Todd, 1999.

Kitwood, Tom. *What Is Human?* London: InterVarsity, 1970.

Kluckhohn, Clyde, and Henry Alexander Murray. "Personality in Nature: The Determinants." In *Personality in Nature, Society, and Culture*, edited by Kluckhohn et al., 35–48. New York: Alfred A. Knopf, 1949.

Konz, D. J. "The Even Greater Commission: Relating the Great Commission to the *Missio Dei*, and Human Agency to Divine Activity, in Mission." *Missiology: An International Review* 46.4 (2018) 333–49.

Kreider, Alan. *The Patient Ferment of the Early Church: The Improbable Rise of Christianity in the Roman Empire*. Grand Rapids: Baker Academic, 2016.

Langmead, Ross. "Refugees as Guests and Hosts: Towards a Theology of Mission among Refugees and Asylum Seekers." *Exchange* 43.1 (2014) 29–47.

Lartey, Emmanuel Y. "Globalization, Internationalization, and Indigenization of Pastoral Care and Counselling." In *Pastoral Care and Counselling: Redefining the Paradigms*, edited by Nancy J. Ramsay, 87–109. Nashville: Abingdon, 2004.

Lartey, Emmanuel Y. *In Living Color: An Intercultural Approach to Pastoral Care and Counselling*. 2nd ed. London: Cassell, 2003.

Lave, Jean, and Etienne Wenger. *Situated Learning: Legitimate Peripheral Participation*. Cambridge: Cambridge University Press, 1991.

Lawrence, Brother. *The Practice of the Presence of God*. 1691. Reprint, Grand Rapids: Fleming H. Revell, 1958.

Lempert, Bex. "Asking Questions of the Data: Memo Writing in the Grounded Theory Tradition." In *The SAGE Handbook of Grounded Theory*, edited by Antony Bryant and Kathy Charmaz, 247–54. Thousand Oaks, CA: SAGE, 2007.

Livermore, David A. *Cultural Intelligence: Improving Your CQ to Engage Our Multicultural World*. Grand Rapids: Baker Academic, 2009.

Longenecker, Bruce. "The Story of the Samaritan and the Innkeeper (Luke 10:30–35): A Study in Character Rehabilitation." *Biblical Interpretation* 17.4 (2009) 422–47.

Macallan, Brian C. *Postfoundationalist Reflections in Practical Theology: A Framework for a Discipline in Flux*. Eugene, OR: Wipf & Stock, 2014.

Malina, Bruce J., and Richard L. Rohrbaugh. *Social-Science Commentary on the Gospel of John*. Minneapolis: Fortress, 1998.

Manzano, Ana, et al. "Active Listening by Hospital Chaplaincy Volunteers: Benefits, Challenges and Good Practice." *Health and Social Care Chaplaincy* 3.2 (2015) 201–21.

Marcel, Gabriel. *The Mystery of Being*. Vol. 1, *Reflection and Mystery*. Chicago: H. Regnery, 1960.

Martin, Judith N. "Revisiting Intercultural Competence: Where to Go from Here." *International Journal of Intercultural Relations* 48 (2015) 6–8.

Meyer, Dale A. "Why Go to Church Every Sunday? Three Reasons from 1 Peter." *Concordia Journal* 45.1 (2019) 8–12.

Miller-McLemore, Bonnie J. "The Human Web: Reflections on the State of Pastoral Theology." *Christian Century* (Apr. 7, 1993) 366–69.

Moreau, A. Scott, et al. *Effective Intercultural Communication: A Christian Perspective*. Encountering Mission. Grand Rapids: Baker Academic, 2014.

Moschella, Mary Clark. "Ethnography." In *The Wiley-Blackwell Companion to Practical Theology*, edited by Bonnie J. Miller-McLemore, 224–33. Chichester, UK: Blackwell, 2012.

"Multicultural Education Programs and Resources." Department of Education, Victoria. https://www.education.vic.gov.au/school/teachers/teachingresources/multicultural/Pages/multidepth.aspx.

"Multicultural Services." Uniting. https://www.unitingvictas.org.au/services/multicultural-services/#:~:text=Contact%20Uniting%20Vic.,we%27ll%20help%20you%20out.

National Centre for Longitudinal Data. *Building a New Life in Australia (BNLA): The Longitudinal Study of Humanitarian Migrants*. Canberra: Australian Government Department of Social Services, 2020. https://www.dss.gov.au/sites/default/files/documents/07_2020/bnla-longitudinal-study-humanitarian-migrants-wave-5.pdf.

Neuger, Christie C. *Counseling Women: A Narrative, Pastoral Approach*. Minneapolis: Fortress, 2001.

Nouwen, Henri. *Reaching Out*. New York: Doubleday, 1975.

BIBLIOGRAPHY

Omohundro, John, T. *Thinking Like an Anthropologist: A Practical Introduction to Cultural Anthropology.* New York: McGraw Hill Professional, 2007.

Palmer, Parker J. *The Active Life: A Spirituality of Work, Creativity, and Caring.* San Francisco: Jossey-Bass, 1990.

———. *A Hidden Wholeness: The Journey Toward an Undivided Life.* San Francisco: Jossey-Bass, 2004.

Paterson, Michael. "Mirror Mirror on the Wall: From Reflective to Transformative Practice." *Health and Social Care Chaplaincy* 1.1 (2013) 67–74.

Pattison, Stephen. "Is Pastoral Care Dead in a Mission-Led Church?" *Practical Theology* 1.1 (2008) 7–10.

Patton, John. *Pastoral Care in Context: An Introduction to Pastoral Care.* Louisville, KY: Westminster John Knox, 1993.

Patton, Michael Quinn. *Qualitative Research and Evaluation Methods.* Thousand Oaks, CA: SAGE, 2015.

Paul VI. "Decree on the Apostolate of the Laity: *Apostolicam Actuositatem.*" Nov. 18, 1965. https://www.vatican.va/archive/hist_councils/ii_vatican_council/documents/vat-ii_decree_19651118_apostolicam-actuositatem_en.html.

Paver, John E. *Theological Reflection and Education for Ministry.* Aldershot, UK: Ashgate, 2006.

Peirce, Charles Sanders. *Collected Papers of Charles Sander Peirce.* Edited by Charles Hartshorne and Paul Weiss. Cambridge, MA: Harvard University Press, 1931.

Pembroke, Neil. *The Art of Listening: Dialogue, Shame, and Pastoral Care.* London: T & T Clark/Handsel, 2002.

———. "Empathic and Compassionate Healthcare as a Christian Spiritual Practice." *Practical Theology* 12.2 (2019) 133–46.

———. *Renewing Pastoral Practice: Trinitarian Perspectives on Pastoral Care and Counselling.* London: Routledge, 2016.

Perry Wallace, Brenda. *Clinical Pastoral Education: A Survival Kit.* CPEO, 2017.

Peterson, Eugene H. *Christ Plays in Ten Thousand Places.* Grand Rapids: Eerdmans, 2005.

———. *Five Smooth Stones for Pastoral Work.* 2nd ed. Grand Rapids: Eerdmans, 1992.

———. Foreword to *Christianity beyond Belief: Following Jesus for the Sake of Others,* by Todd D. Hunter, 9–11. Downers Grove, IL: IVP Academic, 2009.

Ragin, Charles C. *The Comparative Method: Moving Beyond Qualitative and Quantitative Strategies.* Berkeley: University of California Press, 1987.

Ramsay, Nancy, J., ed. *Pastoral Care and Counselling: Redefining the Paradigms.* Nashville: Abingdon, 2004.

"Resources." Baptist Union of Victoria. https://web.archive.org/web/20201024230456/https://www.buv.com.au/resources/multicultural-churches/.

Robinson, David. *Soul Mentoring: Discover the Ancient Art of Caring for Others.* Cambridge: Lutterworth, 2015.

Rohr, Richard. *Everything Belongs: The Gift of Contemplative Prayer.* New York: Crossroad, 2003.

Rooms, Nigel, and Cathy Ross. "Practical Theology and Missiology: Can They Live Together?" *Practical Theology* 7.2 (2014) 144–47.

Ross, Cathy. "Hospitality: It's Surprising What You Hear When You Listen." In *Mission in Marginal Places: The Theory,* edited by Paul Cloke and Mike Pears, 140–56. Milton Keynes, UK: Authentic Media, 2016.

Roxburgh, Alan J. *Joining God, Remaking Church, Changing the World: The New Shape of the Church in Our Time*. New York: Morehouse, 2015.
Roxburgh, Alan J., and Scott M. Boren. *Introducing the Missional Church: What It Is, Why It Matters, How to Become One*. Grand Rapids: Baker, 2009.
Rynkiewich, Michael. *Soul, Self, and Society: A Postmodern Anthropology for Mission in a Postcolonial World*. Eugene, OR: Cascade, 2011.
Schensul, Stephen L., et al. *Initiating Ethnographic Research: A Mixed Methods Approach*. 2nd ed. Plymouth, UK: AltaMira, 2013. Kindle.
Schieb, Karen. "Love as a Starting Point for Theological Reflection." *Pastoral Psychology* 63.5–6 (2014) 705–17.
Schults, F. LeRon. *The Postfoundationalist Task of Theology: Wolfhart Pannenberg and the New Theological Reality*. Grand Rapids: Eerdmans, 1999.
Schwandt, Thomas A. *The SAGE Dictionary of Qualitative Inquiry*. 3rd ed. Thousand Oaks, CA: SAGE, 2007.
Schweitzer, Robert D., et al. "Mental Health of Newly Arrived Burmese Refugees in Australia." *Australian and New Zealand Journal of Psychiatry* (2011) 1–9. http://eprints.qut.edu.au/40622/3/40622.pdf.
Sims, Neil. "A Response to Stephen Pattison: Pastoral Care Integral to Mission." *Practical Theology* 2.2 (2009) 285–86.
Smith, Gordon T. *Spiritual Direction: A Guide to Giving and Receiving Direction*. Downers Grove, IL: InterVarsity, 2014.
Spiritual Care Australia. "Standards of Practice." 2013. https://www.spiritualcareaustralia.org.au/public/103/files/SCA_Standards_of_Practice_Document-1.pdf.
Spiritual Health Association. "About Spiritual Health Association." https://spiritualhealth.org.au/about.
Spitzberg, Brian H. "A Model of Intercultural Communication Competence." In *Intercultural Communication: A Reader*, edited by Larry A Samovar et al., 381–401. Boston: Wadsworth Cengage Learning, 2009.
Sternberg, R. J., and D. K. Detterman. *What Is Intelligence?* Norwood, NJ: Ablex, 1986.
Stone, Bryan P. *Evangelism after Christendom: The Theology and Practice of Christian Witness*. Grand Rapids: Brazos, 2007.
Stott, John. *Christian Mission in the Modern World*. Downers Grove, IL: InterVarsity, 1975.
Strauss, Anselm. *Qualitative Analysis for Social Scientists*. Cambridge: Cambridge University Press, 1999.
Streets, Frederick J. "Love: A Philosophy of Pastoral Care and Counselling." *Verbum et Ecclesia* 35.2 (2014) 1–11.
Streufert, Mary J. "An Affinity for Difference: A Theology of Power." *Currents in Theology and Mission* 37.1 (2010) 28–39.
Stroope, Michael W. *Transcending Mission: The Eclipse of a Modern Tradition*. Downers Grove, IL: IVP Academic, 2017.
Thiessen, Elmer J. *The Ethics of Evangelism: A Philosophical Defense of Proselytizing and Persuasion*. Authentic Media, 2011.
Thompson, Marianne Meye. *John: A Commentary*. Louisville, KY: Westminster John Knox, 2015.
Ting-Toomey, Stella. *Communicating across Cultures*. New York: Guilford, 1999.
Travis, John. "The C1 to C6 Spectrum." *Evangelical Missions Quarterly* 34.4 (1998) 407–8.

BIBLIOGRAPHY

Van Dyne, Linn, et al. "Sub-dimensions of the Four Factor Model of Cultural Intelligence: Expanding the Conceptualization and Measurement of Cultural Intelligence." *Social and Personality Psychology Compass* 6.4 (2012) 295–313.

Volf, Miroslav. *Exclusion and Embrace: A Theological Exploration of Identity, Otherness, and Reconciliation*. Nashville: Abingdon, 1996.

Wade, Geoff. "Australia-China Relations." In Parliamentary Library Briefing Book: 47th Parliament, 272–76. https://www.aph.gov.au/-/media/05_About_Parliament/54_Parliamentary_Depts/544_Parliamentary_Library/Research_Papers/2023-24/Briefing_Book_key_issues_for_the_47th_Parliament.pdf?la=en&hash=8FABC909412711C64771035AA28708E8F34032AC.

Wade, William. "The Emerging Church: From Mission to 'Missional.'" *Journal of Biblical Theology* 1.3 (2016) 217–21.

"What Is Spiritual Companioning (Direction)?" WellSpring Centre. https://www.wellspringcentre.org.au/spiritual-companioning.

Willard, Dallas. "Spiritual Formation as a Natural Part of Salvation." In *Life in the Spirit: Spiritual Formation in Theological Perspective*, edited by Jeffrey P. Greenman and George Kalantzis, 45–60. Downers Grove, IL: InterVarsity, 2010.

Williams, Mark S. "Revisiting the C1–C6 Spectrum in Muslim Contextualization." *Missiology* 39.3 (2011) 335–51.

www.ingramcontent.com/pod-product-compliance
Lightning Source LLC
Chambersburg PA
CBHW071448150426
43191CB00008B/1272